Lone Star Steeples

Number 15: Clayton Wheat Williams Texas Life Series

Publication of this book was supported by a grant from the Today Foundation.

LONE STAR STEEPLES

Historic Places of Worship in Texas

Illustrated by
Carl J. Christensen Jr.

Text by
Pixie Christensen

Foreword by David Ruesink

TEXAS A&M UNIVERSITY PRESS
COLLEGE STATION

First edition

This paper meets the requirements of ANSI/NISO Z39.48–1992 (Permanence of Paper).
Binding materials have been chosen for durability.
Manufactured in China by Everbest Printing Co.
through FCI Print Group
∞

Unless otherwise specified, information on the churches profiled in this book is from The Handbook of Texas Online *(https://tshaonline.org/handbook, published by the Texas State Historical Association) or websites maintained by the churches. See bibliography for complete details.*

Library of Congress Cataloging-in-Publication Data

Names: Christensen, Carl J., Jr., artist. | Christensen, Pixie, writer of added text.
Title: Lone Star steeples: historic places of worship in Texas / illustrated by Carl J. Christensen Jr. ; text by Pixie Christensen; foreword by David Ruesink.
Description: First edition. | College Station: Texas A&M University Press, 2016. | Includes bibliographical references.
Identifiers: LCCN 2015038053| ISBN 9781623493936 (cloth: alk. paper) | ISBN 9781623493943 (ebook)
Subjects: LCSH: Church buildings—Texas—Pictorial works. | Church architecture—Texas—Pictorial works.
Classification: LCC ND1839.C557 A4 2016 | DDC 759.13—dc23 LC record available at http://lccn.loc.gov/2015038053

CONTENTS

Contents

FOREWORD

This book captures the importance of churches that are found in cities and small towns throughout Texas. The beauty and uniqueness of the churches is portrayed by architect and illustrator Carl Christensen Jr. and further explained in the brief historical and architectural descriptions, written by Pixie Christensen, that accompany each of the original watercolor images.

The history of a church usually says something about how folks from a particular country would settle with others from the same country. Which country the immigrants came from often dictated the type and structure for the church. New immigrants often built their church as one of the first community structures after arriving in Texas, and they wanted to retain the flavor of the churches they remembered from their places of origin.

Churches featured in this book have stood for many years, most of them over a century. The original structures still exist for many of them; some are restored either at the same or different places within the community. Some are now closed for weekly services but remain part of the community for special ceremonies. Almost all of the churches have been recognized with a historical plaque by the Texas Historical Commission or the National Register of Historic Places.

The author notes lots of "first" or "oldest" places of worship, such as the first or oldest in the denomination, first with a certain type of architecture, first by a particular architect, and other unique designations. Another striking aspect is how church buildings persevered over time in spite of storms, fire, and often both. As we see the beauty both outside and inside the churches, we gain an understanding of the churches' importance as the communities were being settled. Church buildings were often used for schools right after the church buildings were constructed, showing the importance of the churches to the community for more than just spiritual satisfaction.

Use of local materials, especially soil for bricks, was very common, which accounts for the uniqueness of different church buildings even when they share similar architecture. Sometimes completing the church construction appeared to be part of the call for the clergy who would become the minister of the church (what we might call today a "tentmaker" or a "bi-vocational" minister). In some cases, the minister also helped complete decorating the interior of the structure.

A major theme that runs through the book is the importance of ethnicity in determining what the finished church structure looked like. After reading the book, one may well get an urge to travel the state to see these unique and historic houses of worship.

David Ruesink
Rural Sociology Professor Emeritus
Texas A&M University

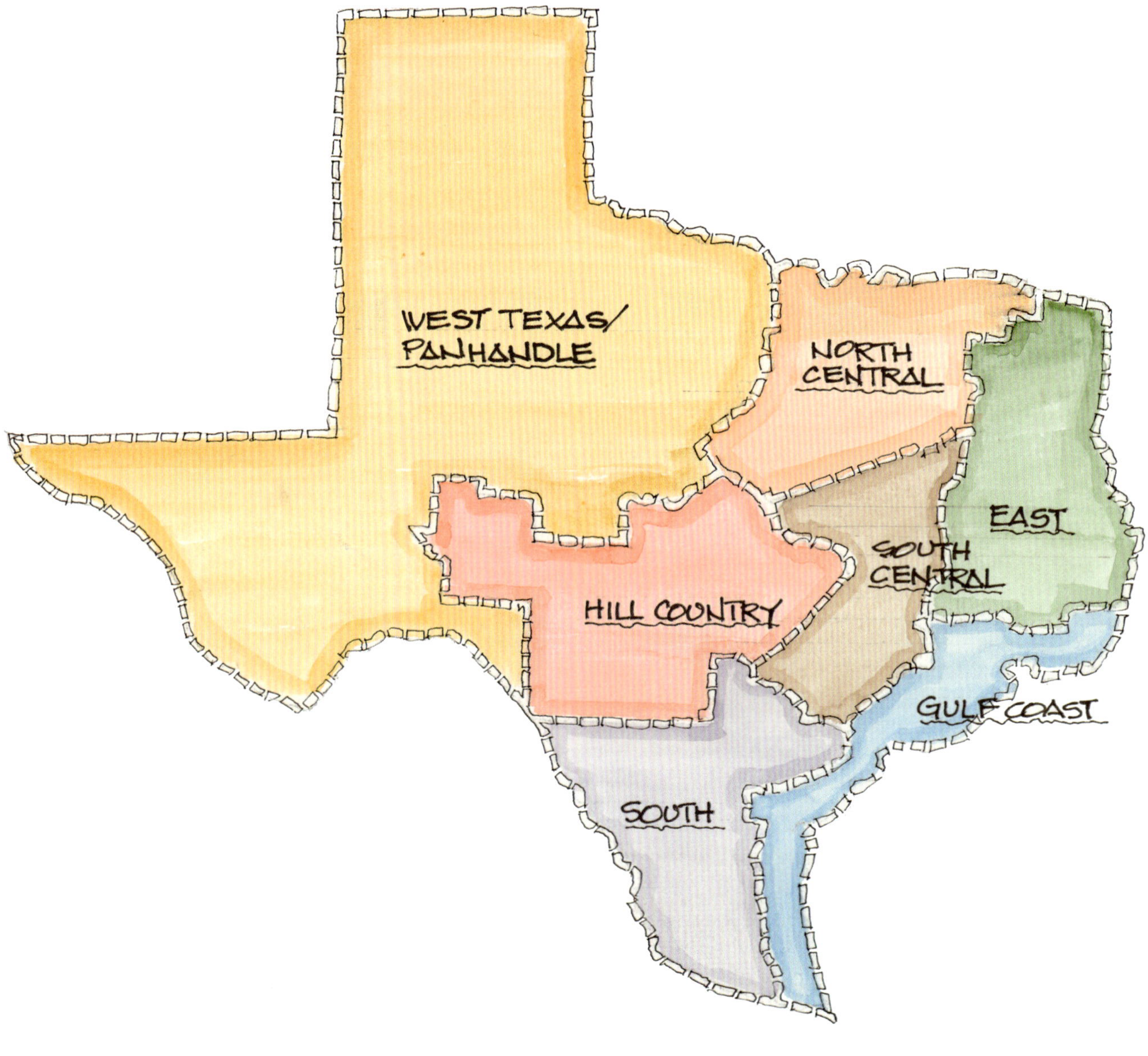
WEST TEXAS/
PANHANDLE
NORTH
CENTRAL
EAST
SOUTH
CENTRAL
HILL COUNTRY
GULF COAST
SOUTH

PREFACE

As the six flags that flew over Texas help define its history, the hundreds of Texas churches recognized by historic markers help define the culture, heritage, religion, and architectural identities of the people of Texas. *Lone Star Steeples* takes the reader on a tour of historic churches across the state. Architectural features, individual stories, cultural markers, and significant events make each church unique and also contribute to the big picture of this big state.

Lone Star Steeples does not pretend to be a comprehensive view of Texas history through its churches; nor does the book claim to represent all architectural styles exhibited by historic churches. But it does offer historic touch points—selected churches that define parts of the state's history and reflect aspects of its varied architecture.

But more than a view of history through church buildings, *Lone Star Steeples* invites the reader to experience the beauty and integrity of each church building through the eyes of the artist/architect who both envisioned and illustrated this book. Carl Christensen Jr. graduated from Texas A&M University with a BA in Architectural Design and an MA in Urban Design. His love of architecture, his appreciation of the function of building design within a community, and his creative art style unite to present these churches as individual pieces of art, documenting the character and story of each unique church building.

The artist's canvas, more than any other medium, communicates the intertwining of the timelessness of faith and the changes wrought by passing time and shifting focus. Each painting tells a story of enduring commitment and of the effects of time, weather, and circumstances surrounding each structure. The artist's eye and thoughtful creation convey the heart and handiwork poured into these structures.

These historic churches represent a variety of architectural styles. From simple clapboard construction and vernacular architecture to Gothic and Romanesque features reminiscent of European cathedrals, the buildings reflect the culture, memories, hopes, and desires of each congregation. European immigrants arrived after weeks on the open seas. They then traveled overland by wagon or oxcart and then on foot to their final destination. What greeted them? Wide-open spaces, Texas thunderstorms and sleet, searing heat and drought, hostile Native Americans, food shortages, and diseases. It was not the "land flowing with milk and honey" that had been romanticized and promised by those promoting the opportunities for a better life. Was it any wonder that the people wanted and needed to immediately establish a church home on which to build a foundation of hope and sustain the memories of the culture and religious traditions they left behind?

The congregants themselves built the churches and found the resources needed—local materials and funding out of their own pockets. There was no question that the building of the church was their job just as much as tending their homes and their farms. There were few building loans or capital campaigns; the people worked together and gave of their resources, financially and physically. These churches represent the personal investments and sacrifices of those who worshipped there. And each building, large or small, reveals much about its people. "All historians seem to agree that they [churches] were the single most important cultural and social force behind the Texas frontier."[1]

While most churches were established to carry on the faith traditions of those who founded them, the early Spanish mission churches were tasked with the role of spreading Christian doctrine among the indigenous inhabitants of Texas while also providing Spain an inroad and claim to the frontier land. The Spanish missions accomplished some of their intended goals, but presented a change in culture and religion for the indigenous people that ultimately did not suit all of the semi-nomadic tribes of Texas. The mission churches did, however, flourish and serve the needs of many other people.

"Spanish colonists erected chapels for their missions, presidios, and secular parishes. The first chapels for the missions were temporary palisaded shelters. However, at the missions that prospered, these were replaced by durable and handsome edifices reflecting the stylistic traditions of Spain and Mexico."[2] The mission chapels served the people—the residents of Mexican Texas. As other colonists arrived in Texas, the need for church construction grew, again fitting the needs of the people. For Anglo-American colonists, that need translated into simple box structures, often of logs or stone, with simple furnishings, handmade from local materials.

Another influence arrived on the frontier scene: the influx of various immigrant groups, each bringing their own form of worship and their own cultural preference and style for church structures. Distinctive architects rose to prominence—Nicholas J. Clayton, James E. Flanders, Leo M. J. Diehlman, to name several. New trends, new building methods and technologies, and growing diverse denominations combined to create an evolving landscape of churches in which the Romanesque and Gothic Revival styles were prominent. Through the various styles, it was the people served by the church who orchestrated the building of the churches, and it was each group's unique cultural, ethnic, and social needs that shaped their churches.

The hope of a better life with opportunities, and in some cases the promise of free land grants, lured immigrants to Texas. Leaving behind their homelands, settlers from Germany, Poland, and other European countries built churches and established homes, clinging to familiar customs and traditions while shaping the Texas landscape with European flavor.

For the German immigrants coming to Texas in the nineteenth century, Texas offered opportunities that Germany could no longer offer. "Social and economic improvement, along with political idealism, were the primary goals for these Texas settlers. Though their goals were practical, they were also responding to the ancient German trait affectionately called Wanderlust, a romantic yearning for exotic distant lands."[3] But the bigger issues of widespread poverty and overpopulation encouraged many Germans to risk everything for the hope of opportunity. Arriving in small groups or singly during the years 1831 to 1845, German settlers sent letters home telling of the available land and freedom.

It wasn't until 1842 with the organization of the *Adelsverein* that the number of Germans arriving jumped to the thousands. The *Adelsverein*, a loosely organized group of noblemen and five princes, wanted to promote German colonization in Texas with the vision of establishing a "New Germany" in America. Despite the hardships, the German settlers continued to arrive, the number reaching nearly thirty thousand by 1860. "In the Hill Country today, more than in any other place in Texas, this European culture from the *Adelsverein* colonists has lingered to the end of the twentieth century."[4] New Braunfels carries the distinction of being the first colonized German village in Texas.

The Germans valued their religion, giving highest priority to building churches in their new communities. For most of these new Texans—Lutherans, Catholics, and German Methodists—it was the church that provided them the stability, cultural identity, and familiar customs to balance the challenges faced by settling the frontier land.

Polish immigration also increased in the 1850s. During that time in Poland, a series of disasters—severe weather, poor economy, lack of food, and typhoid and cholera epidemics—combined to fuel the enthusiasm for choosing Texas. A Polish Franciscan missionary, Leopold Moczygemba, worked to bring one hundred Polish families from the Upper Silesian area of Poland to south-central Texas. Panna Maria, the oldest Polish settlement in the United States and the first Polish Catholic church in the United States, was established, followed by other churches some of which would later be known as the famous "Texas Painted Churches."

Because the language differences created a difficult barrier for assimilation into Texas, the Catholic church in each community served as the center not only for religious services, but also for social activities, including festivals and feasts. For the Poles, the church was everything.

By the time of the Civil War, nearly seven hundred Czechs had arrived in Texas. The chief motivating factor was farmland available at a price they could afford, but they were also motivated by the political and religious oppression in their homeland. The majority of these immigrants followed the Catholic faith, and that carried over in Texas.

"Several independent congregations (the first had been established at Wesley in 1864) were organized into the denomination known as the Unity of the Brethren in 1903, chiefly through the efforts of Rev. Adolf Chlumsky."[5] These Czechs viewed the denomination as a continuation of the traditional Czech religious movement suppressed by the Austrians in the sixteen hundreds. The strong core value of the "Word of God" is foundational to this denomination. Today visitors to the Wesley church can experience this heritage and see expressions of faith through the interior of another of Texas' painted churches.

The memories of religious traditions as well as cultural heritage echo in these historic churches, and the willingness of the congregants to face whatever challenge was thrown their way testifies to the importance of the church in their lives.

Churches played a key role in the lives of African Americans in Texas. In his book *Black Churches in Texas: A Guide to Historic Congregations*,[6] Clyde McQueen noted, "Church houses, from magnificent edifices in Dallas, Houston, and Fort Worth, to the simple, rustic buildings of numerous small communities and rural areas, are the vessels that contain the individual expressions of African American religious faith. Churches are, after all, places of personal worship. But beyond that, they are woven tightly into the social fabric of African American life. Religious beliefs reflect a society's core values—most importantly among African Americans, the values of his family, community, and freedom. For slaves and free persons alike prior to the Civil War, church provided opportunities for social bonding, free from white control."

In East Texas, some slave owners offered separate religious services in their churches for their slaves. Some even built separate churches. Yet others tried to use the church to extend control over their slaves, using religious instruction as a forum for messages on obedience. In a few churches, blacks and whites worshipped together, but for the most part, those churches were led by whites.

According to McQueen, when the Civil War and Emancipation Proclamation granted slaves the independence and freedom to pursue their own interests, for the majority this included establishing their own churches, even their own denominations. The church took on additional roles for the newly freed, in some cases providing educational programs for young black men, helping bridge the transition into independence, and building awareness of political and social opportunities to help African American communities grow.

Congregations met on riverbanks, beneath brush arbors and live oak trees, in log cabins and borrowed space, sharing space with other churches, all the while saving money and working hard to build their own churches. Some of the churches still serve their communities today; some with descendants of the original founders. Some of the churches struggle to keep their doors open, and the telltale signs of deterioration and neglect are obvious. Others have seen their doors reopened with new life through restoration projects and people committed to recognizing the heritage and passing the legacy to future generations.

Some churches have redefined their roles in the community. A church founded and built in Dallas has seen huge demographic changes in its neighborhood. The congregation had to make a choice—stay and serve, or relocate. The "stay and serve" decision created a new role for the church—providing legal services, food banks, and child care for people in the neighborhood—and a new life for the church, providing opportunities for its neighborhood.

Many of Texas' historic churches have been blown down by hurricanes, blown away by tornadoes, or burned to the ground. The wood frames of churches provided easy fuel. But rising even from ashes, many of these churches have lived more than one life. The journey behind *Lone Star Steeples* crisscrossed the state along back roads, farm roads, and state highways. In these journeys and in the stories collected, certain patterns began to emerge: the pride of the people in building their churches debt-free; the perseverance of the people who endured their beloved church being destroyed by natural disaster once, twice, or even three times; and the people's recognition of the church as their cultural foundation, their moral foundation, and their social center.

Lone Star Steeples provides a glimpse of the many cultures and contexts of Texas churches, but the diversity of Texas and its people cannot be covered within the scope of one book. Many more stories are waiting to be told and many more beautiful churches should be portrayed and preserved. We hope this book inspires others to cherish their heritage and tell their stories.

LOST CHURCHES AND ROAD WARRIORS

For all the hours spent in solitude with pen and paint, a book like this couldn't happen without a wide variety of people and a bit of wheels-on-the-road travel. Researching churches usually includes discovering the stories of people involved in those churches, or at least in the church's region. Sometimes the story is the church itself, but we only learn that story through helpful people. Such was the case with Union Missionary Baptist Church in Jefferson. Union Church was definitely on the list for Jefferson churches, but we could not find it. After asking around, it seemed nobody knew where it was located! We tried to follow Google Maps' directions and drove ten to fifteen miles down a country road. A gracious young lady stopped what she was doing to call her mother, a local pastor, to help us in the search. They thought the church was just a few miles farther and off to the left down a dirt road. It turned out to be a church similar in name, but not THE church.

We reluctantly admitted defeat, and in one of those providential moments of just driving through a residential area, we topped a hill and there below us stood the church, the wood frame building resting on concrete blocks and showing years of wear and tear.

Carl explained to the gardener mowing the plush, landscaped yard across the street that we were working on a book of churches. "That one ought to be torn down!" he replied.

But we knew the history of this church, and like so many others we would encounter, we knew the perseverance of the people represented by the church. Union Church rested on cement blocks because a group of people was committed to restoring this historic property.

Union Church helped us define the criteria for churches to be in the book. It quickly became apparent there were many more beautiful historic churches than one book could contain. So how to choose? Union Church defined one selection criterion for us: cultural significance. In each of the geographic areas we chose, we found churches representing cultural and ethnic groups. Geographic area was also key. We followed our adaptation of the division of the state used by *Texas Escapes Online Magazine* (www.texasescapes.com).

Another criterion was historical significance. There are numerous "firsts" and "mosts" within these pages—the first Presbyterian church in the area, the first pipe organ in the city, or the oldest African American church. Historical importance also played a role; did the church play an important role in the settling of an area or in a specific time of Texas history? All but one of the churches has been recognized with either a state or national historical marker.

Variety was important. We wanted to include a broad mix of churches representing size, style, and condition. You'll find chapels and large cathedrals in these pages, some churches deteriorating, others fully restored and in use.

Finally, the trump card was the artist's eye. Maybe the church didn't fit any of our selection criteria but it held a certain beauty or distinction that drew Carl to a box of paints. He just knew he needed to paint that one.

But before the paints came out, there were the road trips. Without countless trips to small towns and big cities, B&Bs and chain motels, local eatery dives and diners, this book would not have been possible. And without the team of fearless and faithful road warriors who joined us on our road trips, the travel would not have been the adventure and fun that it turned out to be. Our thanks to all the road warriors who helped make this possible, both those on the road with us and those we met along the way:

Vic and Bonnie Reid
Tom and Susan Van Wynen
Tom and Bev Woodward
Joel and Barb Trudell
David, Emily, and Baker Christensen
Paul, Chyra, Shane, Shyanne, and Shaylee Christensen
Toby, Keenan, Ian, Grace, and Gillian Fletcher
Mark and Margaret Christensen
Bill and Jana Voigt

Finally, we acknowledge our gratitude to Larry Mitchell for his encouragement during the idea stage of this book and our appreciation of Mary Lenn Dixon and Thom Lemmons for taking that initial idea and guiding it patiently through to completion.

I

Historic Churches of the Texas Gulf Coast

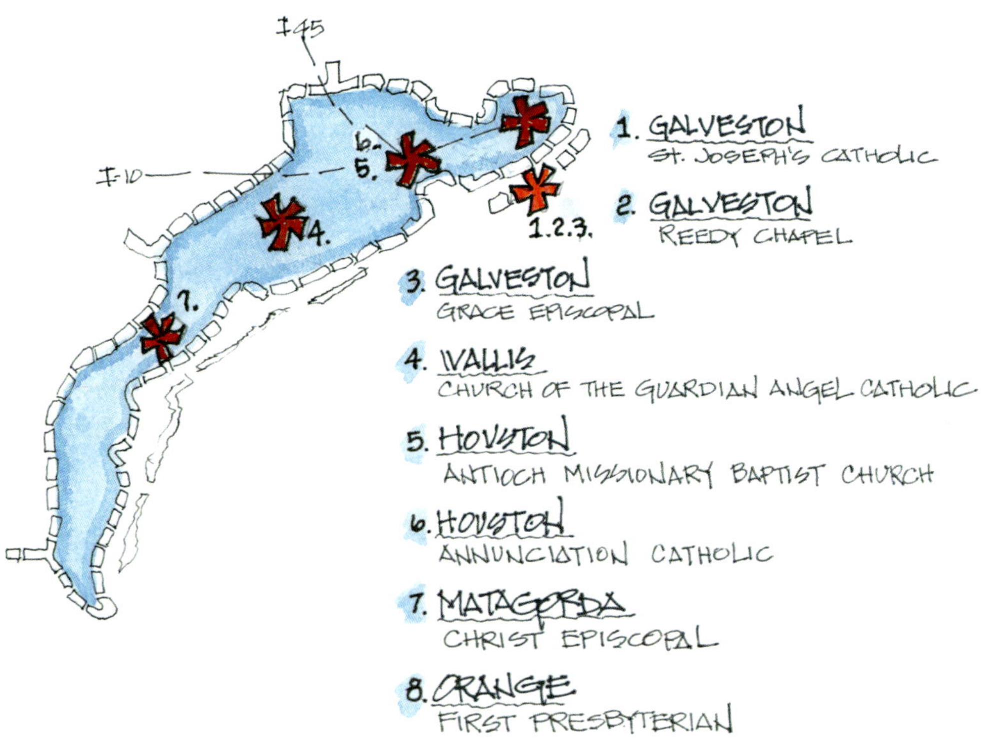

SAINT JOSEPH'S CATHOLIC CHURCH

GALVESTON
Built in 1860
Architect: Joseph Bleicke

If distinguished labels earned a church an award, Saint Joseph's Catholic Church in Galveston would be the worthy recipient. Oldest German Catholic church in Texas; oldest wooden church building in Galveston; one of the four oldest church buildings in Galveston; and one of the few pre-Civil War buildings remaining on Galveston Island—all describe Saint Joseph's Catholic Church.

Hundreds of German immigrants arrived in Galveston in the nineteenth century. Although many settled in towns already established, such as New Braunfels, many others chose to settle on the island that was, at the time, a major port of entry for Texas. When the German population totaled almost half of Galveston's population, Bishop John Odin, first Catholic bishop of Galveston, recommended the construction of a church that would conduct services in German.

Joseph Bleicke, a German architect and immigrant to Galveston, was assigned the job. The new church was dedicated in 1860 and named after the patron saint of laborers, Saint Joseph. The exterior is a simple Gothic Revival style with classical Greek entablature—the upper portion of the church resting on the columns—and Gothic-arched openings. The church has a square bell tower and trefoil window, but the interior features more elaborate detailing: hand-carved altars, painted wood walls, and plaster stations of the cross.

The 1900 hurricane damaged Saint Joseph's, but within a year repairs were completed, keeping much of the original character. Saint Joseph's remained an active parish until 1968, when the Catholic Diocese closed Saint Joseph's and its contents were sold at public auction.

The Galveston Historical Foundation, after learning the planned use of the building was to be a warehouse, leased the church and managed to find and recover most of the original furnishings. Restoration is an ongoing project. Saint Joseph's still stands on a quiet residential corner, guarded by a perimeter of palm trees, witness to the city's history and serving the future of the city as a venue for wedding ceremonies.

cjc Christensen '14

REEDY CHAPEL AFRICAN METHODIST EPISCOPAL CHURCH

GALVESTON
Built in 1863

"History is on Reedy Chapel's side," declared an article in the *Houston Chronicle* in 2008. "It is a history laced with struggle and rebirth." The congregation of Reedy Chapel African Methodist Episcopal Church, located at Twentieth and Broadway in Galveston, changed its name to honor their second pastor, the Reverend Houston Reedy.

Reedy's history began in 1848 with the desire of white slave owners to provide a place of worship for their slaves. Trustees of the Methodist Episcopal Church South purchased the property at Twentieth and Broadway and gave it to the slaves March 18, 1848.

It was at Reedy that General Order Number 3, announcing the end of slavery in Texas, was read. And it was at Reedy where freed men and women found schooling opportunities. Reedy also hosted the first two annual conferences of the African Methodist Episcopal Church, in 1867 and 1868—the "first meeting of Methodist men of color to be conducted by and for African Americans."[1]

The church's first meeting house was built in 1863. Following the Civil War, the church reorganized as the African Methodist Episcopal Church. But in 1870, Methodist Episcopal Church North sued for ownership and took possession of the chapel. Reedy's congregation met in an old soap factory, rented for fifteen dollars per month. Following four years in the courts, the ruling favored the AME Church; the congregation returned to Reedy and assumed the title of "Mother Church" for the AME denomination.

Struggles continued for Reedy. Destroyed by the great Galveston fire of 1885, the church was rebuilt in 1886 only to suffer heavy damage in the 1900 hurricane. More recently, Hurricane Ike battered the church in 2008. In spite of three to four feet of water in the church, priceless pieces survived—a handmade baptismal font, circular chandeliers, the archives room of church history, and one of the oldest pipe organs in Texas.

The organ, built by E. and G. G. Hook and Hastings of New York in 1872, originally belonged to Trinity Episcopal in Galveston. Trinity donated the organ to Reedy in 1930. The organ contains eight hundred pipes with fifteen independent stops and is only one of two organs of its type in the United States. The other organ is in the Smithsonian Institution in Washington.

Today Reedy stands as a testimony to its history, perseverance, and repeated rebirths, still serving the community, still honoring its place in history.

GRACE EPISCOPAL CHURCH

GALVESTON
Built in 1894
Architect: Nicholas Clayton

A refuge, sanctuary, and survivor. Grace Episcopal Church in Galveston has earned all those titles.

Organized in 1874 as a "mission church" of Trinity Episcopal in Galveston, Grace served as Sunday school for children who "lived out in the country"—a few miles across the island. When, in 1884, Henry Rosenberg, wealthy Galveston patron, and his wife Latitia, moved their membership to Grace from Trinity, Grace Episcopal's role emerged as the church it was meant to be.

After Latitia died, Henry married Molly MacGill. Both Henry and Molly were active in numerous civic and charitable activities, including the Rosenberg Library, the Galveston Orphans Home, and seventeen ornate fountains throughout the city. Rosenberg's legacy to Grace was a $30,000 bequest to build a "new" church building.

Nicholas Clayton, architect of several Galveston landmarks, drew up three sets of plans. Molly chose the most simple, and the cornerstone was dedicated December 24, 1894. Built of Texas limestone, Grace exemplifies the "pointed Gothic" style of architecture.

Commissioned by Molly, the reredos, a heavily carved wooden piece behind the altar, have been called "the richest that has ever been put in any church in the south."[2] Depictions representing Matthew, Mark, Luke, and John, as well as fourteen angels, comprise the carving. Midway down on the far right side, the word "sacrifice" is spelled incorrectly, adhering to a custom for artists and craftsmen to include an imperfection in their work as, according to tradition, a testament to the belief that only God is capable of perfection.

During the 1900 hurricane that devastated Galveston Island, a tidal surge forced water into the church. A group of people seeking refuge rode out the storm in the church bell tower. As a sanctuary of hope, Grace hosted the first wedding to take place on the island following the storm, while silt still covered the aisles.

To prevent another catastrophe from a tidal surge, the city was raised as much as seventeen feet. "The work of raising the heavy limestone church was entrusted to a German-born engineer named John Egert, who placed an army of workmen with hand-cranked screw jacks around the base of the church's foundations."[3]

The workmen—moving in union to the beat of a drum—turned each screw jack an eighth of a turn at a time. The entire church was raised without cracking a single stone or stained-glass window. Grace Church stands four-and-a-half feet higher today than when it was built.

Donated by Mr. John A. Harris in memory of the ten members of his family who died in the 1900 storm, the stained-glass windows on the northeast side of the church feature the oleander tree, a plant that blooms almost year round on the island.

Proving its role as survivor, Grace Church again withstood the flood waters of a hurricane—Hurricane Ike in September 2008. With the help of grant funding and dedicated parishioners, Grace not only recovered from the damage, but also restored the original longleaf pine floor in the church that had been hidden under carpet since the 1940s.

CHURCH OF THE GUARDIAN ANGEL

WALLIS
Built in 1915
Architect: Leo Dielman

At the one hundredth anniversary celebration of Guardian Angel Catholic Church, Celebrant Daniel Cardinal DiNardo commended the church body for the "faith, commitment, and sacrifice of the parish founders who built three churches over a period of twenty years, after storms destroyed earlier structures."

Those committed congregants were ten Czech families from Central Texas who moved to Wallis so they could farm.

In 1899, the bishop in Galveston sent the Reverend William Skocek, the first Czech-speaking priest in the area, to minister to the Catholic community in Wallis. The Bishop suggested building a church close to the railroad. Guardian Angel's first building, completed in 1899 and named on Easter Sunday, was destroyed by a tornado in May 1900. Church members, faithfully believing that the name given to the church would prove true, placed their trust in the Lord and moved ahead on a second building.

Before the second building could be completed, the community was again hard hit by the September 1900 hurricane that devastated Galveston. The community's crops were destroyed. Another tornado in June 1901 again destroyed the crops, and also injured and killed several parishioners. The second building was completed in 1904, but by 1912 it was clear the growing parish needed a larger church.

Guardian Angel parishioners had endured crop failures, tornadoes, storms, and yet the seventy-five church families raised nearly $10,000 required for construction to start in 1913 on the third and current building. Designed by architect Leo Dielman of San Antonio, Guardian Angel was built by a local Wallis contractor with the help of volunteers.

A strong hurricane in August 1915 caused extensive damage to the completed church, but the church was blessed, as planned, on October 21, 1915.

Guardian Angel is "one of the last painted churches built in Texas" and "believed to be one of the oldest and largest wood structures of its type in Texas."[4]

Guardian Angel Catholic Church
Wallis, TX
CJC
Carl Christensen '10

ANTIOCH MISSIONARY BAPTIST CHURCH

HOUSTON
Built in 1875
Architect: Richard Allen

Antioch Missionary Baptist Church holds the honor of being Houston's first African American Baptist church and the first brick structure owned by African Americans in Houston.

Organized in January 1866 by nine former slaves and two white Baptist preachers, the church first met in the two preachers' churches—First Baptist Church and the German Baptist Church. Then services were moved to Buffalo Bayou in the "brush arbor" and then to "Baptist Hill," located at Rusk and Bagby streets. Various ministers served the church body until 1868, when John Henry (Jack) Yates, one of Antioch's members, was ordained and became the first minister of the church.

Yates led the church building project in 1875. Richard Allen, African American and former member of the Texas Legislature, designed the red-brick building. As it continued to grow, Antioch's building was enlarged in the 1890s and major alterations were made in the 1930s. The last construction resulted in a Gothic Revival masonry building with steep gables and pointed arch windows and doors.

Antioch played a key role in providing the first educational opportunities for African Americans in the late nineteenth century. Rev. Yates helped found the Baptist Academy, which provided teaching in reading, writing, and arithmetic, as well as training in various trades, and which would ultimately grow to become Texas Southern University. The church remained, throughout the twentieth century, a center for educational, social, and political activities for the African American community.

Today congregants sitting in the original handmade pews can worship against a backdrop of contemporary urban skyscrapers. Antioch continues to serve the community, providing civic, educational, and religious leadership, taking pride in both its historical and current role.

JESUS SAVES

ANNUNCIATION CATHOLIC CHURCH

HOUSTON
Built in 1871
Architect: Nicholas Clayton

Victorian-era architect Nicholas Clayton, known for his elegant churches and prominent buildings in Galveston, including Bishop's Palace, was awarded the contract for Church of the Annunciation in the late 1800s. The church is the oldest existing Catholic church in Houston.

The first Catholic church in Houston, Saint Vincent's, could not keep up with the increasing number of Catholic parishioners. The Reverend Joseph Querat, a canon of the Cathedral in Lyons, France, and a missionary to Texas from 1852 to 1878, agreed with the bishop of Galveston, Claude M. Dubuis, that a larger church was needed. In 1866, Bishop Dubuis purchased the half block of land at Texas and Crawford streets. The price? A mere $2,000! Harris County Courthouse bricks were purchased and used in the church construction.

Clayton designed the church with European cathedral influence, including a dramatic, towering spire and ornate exterior column designs. He designed the bell tower and entrance later. After seeing the plans, parishioners named their sanctuary Church of the Annunciation. The building was dedicated in 1871; six years later, Saint Vincent's closed.

Annunciation's ties to Galveston appeared again after the 1900 hurricane, which destroyed the island city. Saint Vincent's original bell was found among the ruins of Saint Joseph's Church and returned to Annunciation where it remains on display today.

Annunciation still conducts some services in Latin, one of the few Catholic churches to do so.

gChristensen '14

CHRIST EPISCOPAL CHURCH

MATAGORDA
Built in 1841

Deemed the oldest Episcopal church in Texas, Christ Episcopal owes its beginning to the Reverend Caleb S. Ives who was appointed missionary to the Republic of Texas in 1838.

Rev. Ives held the first service of the gathered Episcopalians on Christmas Day and served Holy Eucharist. The church met in a Masonic hall for the first few years while Ives tried to raise money to build a church on a lot donated by Albert Clinton Horton and Abner Lee Clements. When the lumber arrived from New York for the precut church building, Ives didn't have the money to erect it. The lumber sat on the ground for so long that there was concern it would start to rot.

With an additional donation of six hundred acres from Horton, the funds to build were raised. The first church was built, and services celebrated Easter Sunday 1841. A hurricane in 1854 blew the structure over, and the congregation rebuilt four hundred yards west of the original church.

Materials salvaged from the first church, including the altar, communion rail, altar cross, and pews were used in the second building. The original supporting pillars, timbers, flooring, and much of the siding were also all used in the second church. Christ Episcopal's entry is flanked by two round-headed lancet windows. The overall architectural style reflects Italianate and Gothic Revival.

Christ Episcopal Church has endured hurricanes and other challenges, but the work and worship of the church continue to this day.

FIRST PRESBYTERIAN CHURCH

ORANGE
Built in 1912
Architect: James Oliver Hogg

Magnificent, majestic, stately, grand, beautiful, lavish—all describe First Presbyterian Church in Orange, which was built for the purpose of "glorifying God." First Presbyterian claims many unique distinctions.

Granite shipped from Llano, Texas, forms the exterior. The pews and wood paneling in the loft are mahogany, and Carrara marble from Italy adorns the stairs and communion table. The interior dome topped by a copper cupola is rimmed with stained glass. Three prize-winning windows from the 1893 Chicago World's Fair grace the upper foyer, and Lamb Studios of New York provided beautiful leaded art glass windows, made by hand with techniques no longer in use.

First Presbyterian also housed the first air conditioner for a public building west of the Mississippi River. A power plant on the grounds, run by a full-time engineer kept the building cool, which was no small task in the hot, humid climate of Orange.

Designed by architect James Oliver Hogg of Kansas City, Missouri, the church represents modified Greek Revival. The congregation established itself as a church in 1878, and in 1912 the present church, a gift from the Lutcher family of Orange, was completed. Frances Ann Robinson Lutcher oversaw planning for the structure, interior, and finish elements. Mrs. Lutcher never wanted the total cost of the church building to be known. A permanent endowment established by the family maintains the facility to this day.

A Casavant pipe organ, custom-built Martin harpsichord, two grand pianos, and an electric keyboard contribute to the music program in the church worship services. The Casavant organ represents the quality of workmanship and artistry found in the church. The Casavant brothers, following in the footsteps of their father, the first Canadian-born organ builder, built organs for churches around the world. Their reputation soared with the 1891 construction of the organ for the Notre-Dame Basilica of Montreal, an organ with 82 stops.

As the congregation grew over the years, additional buildings met the needs of Christian education for the children and the Presbyterian day school. First Presbyterian serves the community through various social services and programs, including a soup kitchen and summer activities for the children of Orange. Frances Lutcher and her family's legacy to Orange stands firm today in this beautiful church.

CJC
Carl Christensen '15

2

Historic Churches of East Texas

1. NACOGDOCHES
ZION HILL BAPTIST
2. NACOGDOCHES
OLD NORTH CHURCH
3. SAN AUGUSTINE
CHRIST EPISCOPAL
4. SAN AUGUSTINE
JERUSALEM MEMORIAL CME
5. JEFFERSON
CUMBERLAND PRESBYTERIAN
6. JEFFERSON
UNION MISSIONARY BAPTIST
7. PITTSBURG
FIRST METHODIST
8. PITTSBURG
REEVES CHAPEL
9. PITTSBURG
ST. BEULAH CME
10. PALESTINE
SACRED HEART CATHOLIC
11. PALESTINE
FIRST PRESBYTERIAN
12. ATHENS
SHELBY CHAPEL
13. NEW WAVERLY
ST JOSEPH CATHOLIC

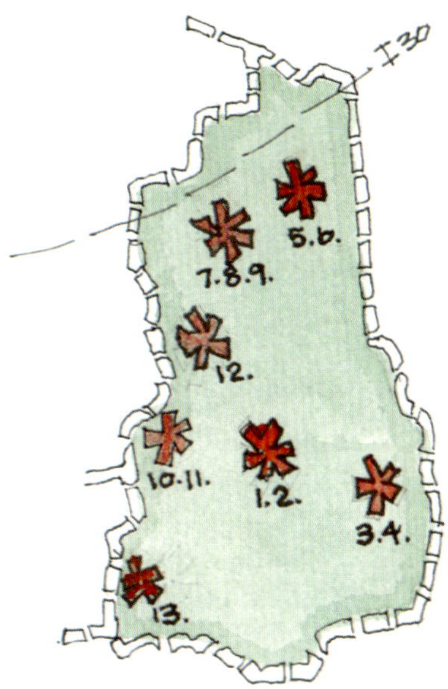

ZION HILL FIRST BAPTIST CHURCH

NACOGDOCHES
Built in 1914
Architect: Dietrich Anton Rulfs

Movement for the eye, numeric symbolism in the window placements, strong Gothic elements of light and towers, historic significance in the area—all are featured in Zion Hill First Baptist Church of Nacogdoches.

The church's first pastor, Lawson Reed, arrived in Nacogdoches in 1878 and found no organized Baptist church for the African American community. He persevered in his desire to start one, and by 1897 the church started meeting regularly under a brush arbor. The congregation grew, and in 1914 a land purchase for a church home was made from a local businessman, John Schmidt.

Schmidt played a pivotal role in the founding of Zion Hill First Baptist Church. He didn't require the church to pay down on the land, and he himself financed the construction. Schmidt wanted to show his appreciation to an African American employee, Charlie Clay, for all the hard work in Schmidt's wholesale grocery store. The congregation occupied the new building in 1914 with J. C. Sweeney as pastor. Dietrich Rulfs, German architect who had designed several residential and business buildings in the city, was hired by Schmidt for the church design.

Representing Gothic architecture blended with Victorian architecture, the six-sided structure and irregular form produce images of motion with architectural elements flowing from one tower to the next, gable to gable, arch to arch. Church symbolism is one characteristic of Gothic architecture, and the number three carries strong symbolism in the Christian church. In Zion Hill, both are played out by three towers, three levels of windows in the arches under the gables, and three trefoils above the windows under the arches.

Zion Hill Baptist faithfully serviced the community for 73 years. In 1987 the church moved to a new sanctuary, and the present building stood vacant and fell into disrepair. Still unoccupied today, it is in a restoration process guided by the City of Nacogdoches.

ZION HILL

OLD NORTH BAPTIST CHURCH

NACOGDOCHES
Built in 1852

"The oldest active missionary Baptist church" in Texas, the Old North Church in Nacogdoches started as a gathering of settlers from various religious denominations. Founding credit goes to Mrs. Massey Sparks Millard, who arrived in Texas in 1832. Historical records cite Mrs. Millard's prayer meeting on the site where the church would eventually be established, a site where she, along with other women and their children, hid in a thicket during Native American and Mexican raids. After that initial meeting, she organized regular prayer meetings for other like-minded settlers.

A group continued to meet near a small post oak tree that was close to a good spring of water. Under Mexican rule, religious freedom was denied those of faiths other than Catholicism, the state religion. The tree served as the "church" building for this small group of believers.

On May 6, 1838, ministers Isaac Reed and Robert G. Green invited people who wanted to constitute a church to come forward. Nine people responded, including two slaves. According to the Texas State Historical Association, "twenty people were baptized at the church in June and July, and were the first Baptist baptisms in East Texas."

The original structure, a log building built in 1838, was named Liberty School House in honor of the Texan victory over the Mexican forces at the Battle of San Jacinto, which won Texas independence. The present church structure was built in 1852 on the foundation stones of the original building.

Current church members celebrate an annual homecoming the first weekend of May, a time for all former and current members to worship together. The famous oak tree succumbed to damage from Hurricane Rita, which struck on September 24, 2005. Tree remnants dot the yard in front of the church building.

Adjacent to the church, the Old North Church cemetery, part of the original ten acres deeded for the establishment of the church, records the early days of Nacogdoches County. Veterans of the American Revolution, the War of 1812, the Texas Revolution, the Civil War, and both world wars are buried there.

CHRIST EPISCOPAL CHURCH

SAN AUGUSTINE
Built in 1870

Frances Cox Henderson, the wife of Texas' first governor, James Pinckney Henderson, was accomplished in many ways—fluent in eighteen languages, involved in civic work and women's suffrage, educated in the law to help run her husband's law office, and credited with establishing individual Episcopalian congregations in East Texas. Christ Church in San Augustine is one of the churches on her list of credits.

In April 1848, at her insistence, the Reverend Henry Samson was assigned missionary work in San Augustine and Nacogdoches. Sadly, the day after his family arrived in San Augustine, his oldest child died of scarlet fever. The child's burial was Rev. Samson's first service, and the child's remains were interred under the church altar.

The original brick Gothic style church was built in 1851. Just eight years later, a storm wrecked the church, destroying the stained-glass windows and the organ. It took ten more years, donated land, and donated lumber and shingles to construct the present day church. The first service in the new building was Christmas in 1870, and Christ Church has been in regular use since. The original rails, hand-hewn pews, and carvings of the Reverend George Crocket are still in the church today.

Described as "one of the more photographed churches in Texas," Christ Church is white frame with an adjoining Gothic bell tower. The tower was added in 1891 to relieve the strain on the building caused by the bell's vibration.

Jerusalem Memorial Christian Methodist Episcopal Church

SAN AUGUSTINE
Built in 1882

Recognized as the oldest black church of record in the state of Texas, Jerusalem Memorial CME Church had its roots in a small one-room house with a round top. The building also served as a school. Two slaves known as Sutton and Bartlett were granted preaching licenses for the Methodist Episcopal Church South in 1845. The congregation called itself "Church on the Branch."

With a strong plantation economy in East Texas, the region counted the highest black population in the state. Some slave owners provided churches for their slaves to attend; some encouraged slaves to attend the same church with them, hoping they could enforce religious instruction focusing on obedience and honesty.

But many African Americans still chose to worship in their own ways, gathering in "hush harbors," clearings in the woods, in churches they were allowed to build by their owners, and in some cases, in their own buildings.

Following the Civil War and Emancipation, most former slaves left the white congregations. Two Methodist denominations in the North—the African Methodist Episcopal Church (AME) and the African Methodist Episcopal Zion Church (AMEZ)—sent missionaries to the area to encourage church growth.

"In 1866 the Methodist Episcopal Church South formed a separate conference for its black members, known as the Colored Methodist Episcopal (CME) Church," according to a historical marker at the church. "The San Augustine 'Church on the Branch' joined the conference in 1870 under the pastorate of the Rev. Sam Horton but was not officially known as Jerusalem CME Church until 1946."

At the yearly CME conference in 1954, members voted to change the name from Colored Methodist Episcopal Church to Christian Methodist Episcopal Church. Jerusalem CME Church still serves a congregation today after more than one hundred years serving the community and helping in the growth of Methodism in San Augustine.

Carl Christensen 12

Cumberland Presbyterian Church

JEFFERSON
Built in 1872
Architect: John Ligon

Standing tall, large, and distinguished, the Cumberland Presbyterian Church (formerly known as First Presbyterian Church) in Jefferson once mirrored the prosperous town at the height of the steamboat era and once boasted the largest congregation in Texas.

John Ligon is the architect of record, but the church bears a strong influence from Plate Ninety-One of George Bowler's book *Chapel and Church Architecture*.[1] Numerous publications on church architecture served communities well in the late nineteenth century. Books on church plans provided building schemes for many rural communities, and also provided creative ideas to architects and church boards in urban areas.

Cumberland's distinctive use of local brick made on site and used in a variety of ways reflected both Gothic and Renaissance design, creating a unique look. The exterior entry staircase, made of iron, emphasized the advance of technology and mass-produced elements into church building.

Positioned facing the central market square, the church appealed to the city council for help in putting a clock in the clock tower, visible for all.

The council agreed, and construction proceeded. But before the clock could be added to the tower, the once prosperous city took a financial hit from the removal of the "Great Red River Raft," a massive log jam that had allowed the water level on Caddo Lake and Big Cypress Bayou to support steamship travel. Once the water table dropped, and Jefferson's population began to dwindle, the city council could not fulfill its commitment. Painted clock faces on the sheet metal, marking the time of worship services, completed the clock tower.

Full restoration of the church began in 1989. Where sanctuary windows had been knocked out, pigeons had chosen the church sanctuary as home. But today the sanctuary is again in use, and still houses the original 1872 lectern, fern stands, pews, and children's chairs for Sunday school classes.

CJC
Carl Christensen '15

UNION MISSIONARY BAPTIST CHURCH

JEFFERSON
Built in 1883

Seeing Union Missionary Baptist Church as it is today, standing in a Jefferson residential neighborhood with rotting wood and peeling paint, denies the rich heritage and cultural role of this church in the history of East Texas.

A Jefferson settler and mayor, Capt. William Perry, donated the property for the church in 1842 to the local slaves for a place of worship. Union Church is considered one of the oldest black churches in Texas.

Following the Civil War, the church witnessed uncertainty and at times violence during the period of Reconstruction. One night a gang of men killed a man outside of town, and then proceeded to the church, with the intent to burn it down. Unknown to them, some of the congregation's freedmen were huddled inside determined to protect their church. They fired their guns to chase the men away.

Several nights later the gang returned, and the church structure was destroyed by fire. The church building standing today was finished after federal troops left Jefferson in 1871. Tradition holds that the church was built of cypress trees native of the area. As it witnessed the time of Reconstruction, the church also experienced the civil rights movement and the era of integration. At one time, Union Church hosted every special religious event for African Americans in the area. But as time passed, the congregation grew inactive. Members left; old members passed away. The church bell that once rang to announce worship now stands silent. But if Tommie L. Jackson has his way, that bell will ring again, to celebrate weddings, family reunions, and other special events.

Jackson remembers well how he rang the bell as a youngster, calling the church parishioners to morning services. One of his jobs was to clean the church, for two dollars a week. One of his ancestors was one of the original congregants.

In October 2011, Union Missionary Baptist Church was filled with people again, gathered to celebrate the church's 169 years of service to the community. The day also marked the official start of a capital campaign to raise funds to restore the church to its 1883 condition. "A nonprofit organization consisting of congregation members [including Jackson] and other interested parties, including the Collins Foundation—a historic preservation organization in Jefferson—are now spearheading the efforts to restore the church and preserve its African American heritage."[2]

Union Church, witness to history and participant in social change, may stand in disarray now, but not disrespect.

WELCOME
TO
UNION E.C.
CJC
Carl Christensen '13

CJC
Carl Christensen '13

FIRST UNITED METHODIST CHURCH

PITTSBURG
Built in 1905
Architect: James E. Flanders

With the combined help of architect James E. Flanders (1849–1928) and the rapid growth of Pittsburg's business district and its conversion from wood buildings to brick, First United Methodist Church boasts a blend of Gothic and Prairie style architecture. The hard-finished orange brick stands out in the sea of traditional red-brick church edifices.

The church itself was organized in the late summer of 1867, and congregants met in a log building. A two-story wooden structure replaced that building, but it was clear with the growth of the congregation that a new structure was needed. Flanders designed the church building in 1904; construction was completed in 1905. Construction cost was a mere $25,000. According to church lore, minutes before the church dedication, local banker R. A. "Lon" Morris made a last minute contribution of $8,000 to ensure construction expenses were covered.

The stained-glass windows, made in St. Louis, cost $2,650. The stained-glass windows and solid oak woodwork have all been carefully preserved, promising future congregants and visitors that the beauty of the church building will remain.

Horizontal bands around the top of the church towers exemplify Prairie School architecture. At First Methodist, the bands are filled with decorative plaster (see detail sketch). Flanders designed three other Prairie School Gothic churches in Texas: Trinity Methodist in Dallas (destroyed by fire in 1985), Saint John's Methodist Church of Stamford, and First Methodist Church in Royse City.

REEVES CHAPEL

NEAR PITTSBURG
Built in 1905

If you ask for directions to Reeves Chapel, you may hear, "Oh it's on the way to Ferndale," or "Just turn at the mortuary and go a couple of miles and then turn again on Farm Road 1590." Set apart from the town of Pittsburg, Reeves Chapel offers another unique look at Texas settlers.

It was the lack of a cemetery that prompted the founding of Reeves Chapel. In the 1850s, the area just four miles southwest of Pittsburg was settled by a family from Georgia. Another Georgia man, Counce Reeves, Civil War veteran, also chose the area to buy farmland. The dense, forested land must have reminded them of their home state. When Reeves was clearing the land, a tree fell on a migrant worker, killing him.

When Reeves realized there was no proper place to bury the worker, he and his wife donated two acres of their land for a cemetery and adjacent church. The community of settlers then assumed the name of Reeves Chapel.

Organized by the Reverend D. Dane of Jefferson, the congregation of Reeves Chapel Methodist Church first erected a brush arbor to identify their meeting place. Then, they built a thirty-by-sixty-foot structure. It served the community until 1905 when it was replaced with a more elaborate structure still standing today.

Driving down Farm to Market Road 1590, you'll find Reeves Chapel standing vigil in the curve of a winding country road. Trees still surround the two acres, and the adjoining cemetery quietly marks the passing of settlers and citizens, veterans and families, all laid to rest in quiet homage to the migrant worker who died clearing the land.

Carl Christensen '12

SAINT BEULAH CHRISTIAN METHODIST EPISCOPAL CHURCH

PITTSBURG
Built in 1896

Saint Beulah Christian Methodist Episcopal Church was recognized by the Texas Historical Commission and awarded an official historical marker in 1985. The white wood-frame building is a model of Gothic Revival-style architecture.

Congregation members donated the stained-glass lancet windows. A typical element of Gothic ecclesiastical buildings, lancet windows are generally tall and narrow with a pointed arch at the top resembling a lance.

Rev. Joseph Lloyd, who arrived in Pittsburg sometime between 1870 and 1889, organized the church. Construction of the church was completed in 1896, and the name Saint Beulah was chosen at that time. Beulah is a Hebrew name meaning "bride." In John Bunyan's book *The Pilgrim's Progress*, Beulah is the Promised Land. American spirituals often referred to "Beulah land" meaning Heaven.

Saint Beulah is still an active church today.

SACRED HEART CATHOLIC CHURCH

PALESTINE
Built in 1893
Architect: Nicholas J. Clayton

The City of Palestine hosted the state firemen's convention in 1890. Even with all the firemen in attendance, the wooden structure of Saint Joseph's Catholic Church burned to the ground. Saint Joseph, the patron saint of workingmen, was a fitting name for the church built in 1873 on land donated by the International-Great Northern Railroad.

But if Saint Joseph's had not burned to the ground, Nicholas J. Clayton, architect, would not have had the opportunity to design the present church, Sacred Heart. Clayton, known for his design of the Bishop's Palace in Galveston, was considered "among the most noteworthy Roman Catholic architects of nineteenth-century Texas."[3] Clayton excelled in intricate detailing and beautiful composition while respecting not only the values of the period but also the spiritual sensitivities of the individual congregation.

Sacred Heart was made from 675,000 bricks baked on site from Trinity River mud. The Victorian Gothic-style building features stained-glass windows from Italy and France. Its interior altar is encompassed by decorative windows and *The Transfiguration of Christ* mural, painted in the 1920s. The original wood altar was replaced with a marble altar in 1935.

Masses in English and Spanish are held at Sacred Heart, a church still serving the community as it did when it was founded.

CJC
Carl Christensen

FIRST PRESBYTERIAN CHURCH

PALESTINE
Built in 1888
Architect: Dodson and Dudley

Palestine's First Presbyterian Church boasted several firsts in the city: first church bazaar, first church wired for electricity, first church building with glass windows, and first pipe organ.

Formed in November 1849 with the help of the Reverend John Becton and the Reverend Daniel Baker, the eighteen men and women requesting a Presbyterian church relied on Becton as a circuit rider who agreed to come to Palestine every two to three months.

The first church building was constructed of handmade bricks in 1854 with the help of male congregants. Not content with unplastered interior walls, the ladies of the church organized Palestine's first church fair and bazaar. The women raised $350, enough to plaster the interior walls and to purchase a church bell. That same bell still rings from the church tower today.

As the town grew, the church expanded. Moving from its original site to a nearby lot, the cornerstone for a new church was laid July 12, 1888. The architectural firm of Dodson and Dudley oversaw building by Joseph Frederick Wolff. Wolff also operated the local brick plant, producing bricks fashioned from the local heavy, red clay.

The church is built in the Gothic style with Tiffany memorial windows. Even though the church's move placed it in the center of a city block, the church's corner tower with a tall slender steeple was clearly visible. The original contractor was unable to put the steeple up, and for more than a year the church went without.

The story of the steeple is told in Jack Selden's book, *Seven Score and Ten, One Hundred Fifty Years of The Presbyterian Church in Palestine, Texas,* in which Selden quoted J. U. "Shorty" Maffitt, the owner of a local clothing store. "My dad (C. S. Maffitt) came to Texas from Black Mountain, North Carolina, in 1887. . . . He came down to Palestine as it was booming. That was 1888 the year the Presbyterian present church was built. The contractor on the church was unable to put the steeple up. . . . My dad heard about it and made an agreement with the church people to erect the steeple. They did not think he could do it, but they gave him the job anyway. Well, he erected the steeple as he agreed to and it stands to this day."[4]

In 1904 the congregation wanted a pipe organ. The Ladies Aid Society undertook the task of funding the purchase and succeeded in raising nearly half the amount needed. One of the church elders wrote a family friend asking for some help. A note from that friend, Andrew Carnegie, now framed and sitting on the table in the church parlor, informed the elder of Carnegie's contribution of $1,250.

First Presbyterian holds the distinction of being the oldest church building in Palestine continuously serving a congregation.

cjc
Carl Christensen 13

CJC
Carl Christensen 12

cjc
Carl Christensen '13

SHELBY CHAPEL

OUTSIDE ATHENS
Built in 1895

Unassuming in its edifice and humble in its surroundings, the Shelby Chapel traces the descendants of James Madison Shelby who settled in Texas in the 1870s. A native of North Carolina, Shelby moved his large family to Texas from Alabama and established a Presbyterian church, Morrison Chapel, named after the minister at the time.

Church members met in the home of James and Amanda Shelby. It was Amanda who later donated seven acres of land to her daughter and son-in-law, reserving two acres for a Presbyterian church and cemetery. Contract for construction of the chapel, to be called Shelby Chapel, was awarded to Thomas Dunklin, another Shelby son-in-law, in 1895.

Shelby Chapel's simple construction carried over a tradition common among evangelical churches in the mid-nineteenth century—having two entrance doors that were identical and side-by-side, providing one entrance for women, one for men.

According to a 1986 Kentucky study of rural churches in Callaway County, Missouri, the "tradition of providing separate entrances for men and women grew out of changes in Protestant worship rituals and the growing significance of women to the frontier church. The frontier church's dependence on volunteer contributions and participation created specialized tasks. Women inherited many of these and had therefore, an opportunity to exercise leadership and to attain status in frontier communities."[5]

James Madison Shelby, Amanda Shelby, and other Shelby family members were interred at Shelby Chapel's adjoining cemetery. The final home also for many armed forces veterans, including Confederate soldiers, the cemetery documented not only the area settlers, but also the role of a frontier church.

SAINT JOSEPH CATHOLIC CHURCH

NEW WAVERLY
Built in 1905
Architect: L. S. Green

The story of Saint Joseph Catholic Church builds on the history of Polish immigration to Texas. Formed by a group of Waverly planters, the Waverly Emigration Society, with the help of a Polish merchant and his connections in Poland, imported laborers in 1866 to work their farms. The following summer forty Polish families arrived, committed to the American dream to work hard and eventually become land owners.

Rev. Felix Orzechowski was sent to the area by the bishop of the Diocese of Galveston to take care of the Polish people, and Saint Joseph's was birthed from the gathering of these Polish families around Old Waverly and Huntsville.

A Texas historical marker at the church describes the priest's role: "The Rev. Felix Orzechowski, who came to Texas in 1866 to answer an appeal for Polish missionaries, organized Saint Joseph's parish in 1869, the first Catholic church in Walker County. Rev. Orzechowski served the parishioners in their homes or in outdoor services."

The first actual church building, overseen by Rev. Victor Lilnnicki, Rev. Orzechowski's successor, was about twenty by thirty feet, a box-house construction. A second church building in 1892 met the need of the growing parish. A Chicago publishing firm donated the main altar, and a local family donated the lumber.

The present church, built in 1905, addressed the desire of the new priest, Father Thomas A. Bily, to build a church as a "thanksgiving by the people of Saint Joseph's for having been brought together into a successful community, for having been given a parish, and for having been allowed to live as a free people in a great country."[6]

Built to model a cathedral, the Gothic structure has a vaulted, sixty-foot ceiling and cruciform edifice of 120 feet by sixty feet. The men and women had designated sides for seating, a tradition followed through the 1950s. The men's pews had hat clips along the back, and the women's pews had hooks for purses. Wood and plaster dominate the interior, with varnished wainscot meeting the painted plaster four feet from the floor. A storm in the 1940s destroyed the large stained-glass window originally in the bell tower. The window was finally replaced during a 1986 restoration.

The 1892 church building was made into a school and living quarters for the resident nuns. Father Bily served at Saint Joseph's for nineteen years. He died as he walked into the school one morning, and church legend holds that the church's clock face, painted with the time of 11:25, marked the time of his death.

Today, New Waverly Church counts more than six hundred families of diverse backgrounds. Mass is conducted in English and Spanish. Saint Joseph's is recognized as the "mother" of all Polish settlements in Texas.

CJC
Carl Christensen 12

3

Historic Churches of North Central Texas

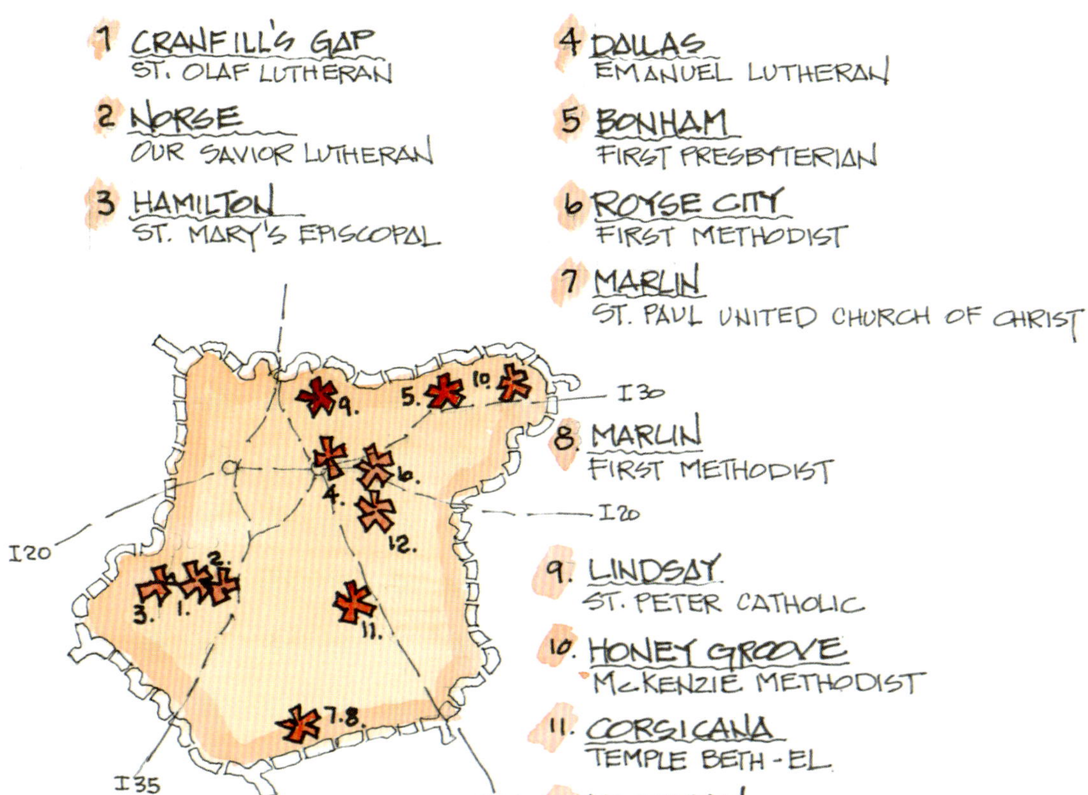

SAINT OLAF LUTHERAN CHURCH

CRANFILLS GAP
Built in 1886
Architect: Andrew Michelson

"Both religion and architecture provided a sense of stability, emotional security, and social continuity to immigrants."[1] Saint Olaf Lutheran Church, known today as the Old Rock Church, near Cranfills Gap aptly fit that description for the Norwegian settlers in Bosque County.

Established in the 1840s by Ole Canuteson, a farmer from Illinois, the settlement grew to be the largest Norwegian community in Texas. But the story of Norwegians immigrating to Texas relies more heavily on Cleng Peerson, one of the early Norwegian immigrant scouts. Peerson made a three-year journey investigating various settlement options on behalf of Quakers who suffered religious persecution in his home country. The first group of fifty-three immigrants arrived in 1825 in New York. Peerson then explored more territory in the Midwest, and in 1849 Peerson journeyed to Texas to evaluate the land and conditions.

Free land and economic opportunities, as well as religious freedom, lured Norwegian immigrants. His enthusiasm for Texas as well as the offering of some of his own land from a 320-acre free grant drew a small group of his countrymen. Even with the opportunities available, compared to Norway, Texas challenged the new settlers with hot weather, scarce water, Native Americans, disease (malaria), and "everything else that stings and bites."[2]

Designed and built by Andrew Michelson and brothers Christian and Ole Canuteson, the Old Rock Church exemplifies the characteristic design for rural ethnic European churches—a gabled oblong box with a belfry in the center of the box. Local farmers helped with the quarrying of native limestone two miles from the church site. The church bell, weighing 3,200 pounds, was hauled into place, and the remaining construction for the steeple area was completed around it.

The carved wooden reredos, a standalone screen with a full-figure painting of Christ, stands behind the altar. One result of a restoration project in 2010 was moving the altar back to its original position when the church was built, directly in front of the reredos.

With strong ties to its Norwegian heritage, the church and nearby community retained use of Norwegian as the primary language well into the 1900s. Today the church, standing alone on a rise above Meridian Creek valley, marks special celebrations only.

Around 2008, an architectural firm noted for restoration took on the church. More than $200,000 was spent in church restoration, restoring the colors inside and out close to the original. Work was also done on the exterior to expose the original rock.

CJC
Carl Christensen '12

OUR SAVIOR'S LUTHERAN CHURCH

NORSE
Built in 1876

After thirty years of establishing Norwegian communities throughout the United States, Cleng Peerson, father of Norwegian immigration to America, finally settled in Bosque County. Eventually he was joined by thousands of Norwegian settlers, creating the largest Norwegian community in the Southwest.

During the early colonization, the city of Norse served as the heart of the settlement. Today the area is called the Norse Historic District, established by the Department of the Interior in 1983. Little remains of the once-thriving community except the historic church and the cemetery where Peerson is buried.

Our Savior's Lutheran Church was organized in 1869 and the wooden church building completed in 1876. As the community continued to grow, a second church was built in Cranfills Gap called Saint Olaf, known today as the Old Rock Church. Norway's King Olaf visited Our Savior's Church and cemetery in 1982 to commemorate the two hundredth anniversary of the birth of Peerson and honor his accomplishments.

Our Savior's Lutheran contains the original chancel furniture, and the interior has remained, for the most part, unchanged except for new pews and carpet. Exterior walls were brick veneered in 1907 and then re-bricked in 1956 to strengthen the structure.

Today, Our Savior's continues as an active church, honoring Norwegian customs throughout the year including Norwegian Constitution Day in May, smorgasbord in November, and Norwegian Country Christmas and Lutefisk Dinner on the third Saturday in December.

CJC
Carl Christensen

SAINT MARY'S EPISCOPAL CHURCH

HAMILTON
Built in 1891

Dancing in the small-town Texas church during the 1940s? A story told about Saint Mary's reports on a dance in the church parsonage, sponsored by the USO. Town citizens were shocked that the church would host the dancing.

Saint Mary's Episcopal Church started in 1868 in the home of Mrs. E. D. Bell, an "earnest church woman." The first itinerant pastor to serve the group of Episcopalians, the Reverend Alexander Gregg, rode from Galveston on horseback.

At Mrs. Bell's request, Bishop Alexander C. Garrett made his first visit in 1875. "If it had not been for Mrs. Bell," Garrett reported, "I would never have found Hamilton," whose nearest railroad point was Texas Central, twenty-one miles away.[3] As more settlers began to arrive in Hamilton, Bishop Garrett scheduled regular visits throughout the year.

The formation of the Ladies Guild in 1888 proved to be a turning point for the future of the church. The guild's first project was to raise money for a building, and within two years, the money was in hand. With a lot donated by Major C. W. Cotton and an altar, seats, and ornaments donated by a leading businessman, the carpenter Gothic church opened its doors in 1891.

Saint Mary's, the first Episcopal church in Hamilton County, is the oldest church to remain on its original location in the city. Its interior woodwork testifies to the craftsmanship of the original carpenters. The interior wood details include tongue-in-groove boards arranged in orderly geometric patterns.

EMANUEL LUTHERAN CHURCH

DALLAS
Built in 1906

Emanuel Lutheran Church at the corner of Peak and San Jacinto streets in Dallas stands unique among the Evangelical Lutheran Churches of America due to its age, its diversity, and its focus on ministering to the inner city. In 1956, fifty years after its founding, the congregation faced a decision: stay at the East Dallas location even though the face of the neighborhood had changed over the years, or move to a different location.

Their decision to stay created a name within the community, "the church with the red door." It's the church with the red door that ministers to the neighborhood in a variety of ways, including a food pantry, childcare, and legal services. Families living in the area know help is available at the church with the red door.

In 1906, a small group of Swedish immigrants founded Emanuel Lutheran. The church building itself came together in phases, with hands-on participation and building by the church congregants. Today its members come from all over the Dallas area, regularly attending the church's first service. The second service serves the families in the neighborhood.

"Emanuel has evolved to serve its ever-changing community over the years. . . . Worship in the beautiful little sanctuary has been celebrated in the language of the community, starting with Swedish, moving to English, adding a Spanish-language service in 1975," according to the church's website. "In the 1980s Emanuel was blessed with Asian refugees living in the neighborhood, and for a while the gospel was heard in Vietnamese and Cambodian."

Today the neighborhood continues to change. Emanuel Lutheran serves as it was founded, with hands-on participation.

FIRST PRESBYTERIAN CHURCH

BONHAM
Built in 1885

In 1885, when Bonham's First Presbyterian Church was built, mass production and railroad transportation partnered to provide rural churches access to building materials—materials that offered creative and aesthetic options.

First Presbyterian represents carpenter Gothic architecture—incorporating Gothic elements while using local materials, especially wood. Mass production enabled the church builders to incorporate sheet-metal shingles, stained glass, and factory woodwork and trim.

The church's original Mohler organ, installed in 1912, was a free-standing pedal organ. One of the pastor's children, Thel Williams, helped pump the organ for his mother, Emile, the church organist. With electric bellows added in 1964, the organ remains one of Bonham's two pipe organs.

Throughout the years, First Presbyterian's dedicated congregation maintained and remodeled the church with respect to its heritage. The commitment of the congregation is clearly spelled out on the church website: "As members and staff of the church we are inheritors of this building, this gathering place. Those who came before us built and established this space, creating a building that has lasted over 120 years." The state historic marker at the church is simply worded: "Only church in the area with a spire and a belfry."[4]

Carl Christensen '13

FIRST UNITED METHODIST CHURCH

ROYSE CITY
Built in 1904
Architect: J. E. Flanders

The official state historical marker for First United Methodist Church in Royse City describes the church architecture in this way: "J. E. Flanders, a well-known Dallas architect, designed the frame structure with three prominent entry towers and decorative shingling." Flanders was known for his Methodist church designs characterized by the use of towers. The Royse City church exemplified Western Gothic architecture—a style that copied the Gothic cathedrals of Europe with one main exception—the structure was built of wood, not stone.

The three towers of the Royse City church place it in the category of Trinity Western Gothic, with each of the towers representing one part of the trinity—God the Father, God the Son, God the Holy Spirit. The crosses, each with four symbols, that top each tower point to the four gospels. Also following Gothic tradition, the sanctuary is built in the form of a cross with the nave (the central part of the church where the congregation is seated) running east and west.

Also characteristic of Gothic tradition are the arched stained-glass windows. Most pure Gothic churches include rose windows and arched windows, but Western Gothic moved toward more artistic glasswork.

The church had its start in 1887 when a group of settlers met in a school house and organized the church. Descendants of those settlers are still active in the church. First United Methodist Church was the first church built in Royse City, with the construction rushed so it could be completed in time for a wedding. By 1904, the church had outgrown its building, and the second church was built, the building still in use today.

SAINT PAUL UNITED CHURCH OF CHRIST

MARLIN
Built in 1920

German settlers organized the Saint Paul Evangelical Lutheran Congregation in 1894. Reverend F. W. Ernst Hartmann led the church. In 1896 the congregants built a school, and the first resident minister, Rev. Dr. Samuel D. Press, later became head of Eden Seminary in St. Louis.

The present church building, replacing the original building that was struck by lightning in 1914, was completed in 1920. The structure was built in a double-gable form used by Evangelical Protestants at the end of the nineteenth century and early twentieth century. The frame church has gables that face to the front and side, as well as a dominant tower in asymmetrical composition. The entrance door is part of the tower. The Saint Paul Church officially changed its name to Saint Paul United Church of Christ in 1957 with the merger of several denominations.

"In 1999, five years beyond its centennial, Saint Paul had only seventy-five members, all belonging through birth or marriage to one of three core family groups," recount Lois E. Myers and Rebecca Sharpless in their book, *Rock Beneath the Sand, Country Churches in Texas*. "Older members remembered days gone by, between the world wars, when the church and its neighborhood reached their population peak." At its peak, Saint Paul, like many churches of that era, served as the hub of social activity for church members.

Saint Paul Church maintains weekly worship services and continues to help preserve the heritage of German immigrants to Texas.

cjchristensen '13

FIRST UNITED METHODIST CHURCH

MARLIN
Built in 1910
Architect: J. E. Flanders

Before the formal establishment of Marlin as a city, Methodist circuit riders served the people in the area. The first, the Reverend John W. DeVilbiss, arrived in 1842. Others followed until 1874 when the Reverend Charles Brown received the appointment as full-time pastor of the Methodist congregation.

The Methodists selected a lot for a church building in 1851, adding adjoining lots in 1879 and 1881, but it wasn't until May 1908 that the church building committee organized and held its first meeting. James Edward Flanders, a church architect from Dallas, submitted design sketches; the committee accepted them in February. The cornerstone was laid in March 1910, with completion of the church in September.

Flanders's church design had already been followed by the Methodist church in Mangum, Oklahoma, built the year before. The Marlin church was the only documented example of a duplicate church building from Flanders's plans.

The church exterior exhibited red bricks, made from clay from the Brazos River bottom. The upper towers were covered with plaster and terra-cotta panels. Italian stained-glass windows accented the front.

First United Methodist represents one of Flanders's church designs in which he adapted the Akron Plan characterized by a large open space or "rotunda" surrounded by classrooms. Sliding doors allowed the rotunda to open to the classrooms. The combination of preaching and education paved the way for Sunday schools and offered local churches the opportunity to educate poor children in the community. Methodist churches, especially, led church denominations in promoting Sunday schools.

Still an active church today, First United Methodist remains one of Flanders's finest surviving churches.

SAINT PETER CATHOLIC CHURCH

LINDSAY
Built in 1918
Architect: Frank A. Ludewig

"The truths of the Catholic Faith are handed down to each successive generation, and with the heritage of Faith, the responsibility of caring for the church in which the Faith is manifested and sustained."[5] From their first celebration of mass as a congregation, the members of Saint Peter Catholic Church in Lindsay dutifully accepted their role to care for and sustain the church. Anton Flusche hosted that first mass for the German colonists in his home on March 25, 1892.

The Germans built a small frame church, and even on Sundays when no priest was available, the colonists still met to say rosary. Responsibility for Saint Peter's religious duties passed to the Benedictine Fathers of Arkansas in 1899; several years later a brick church was built, a church the congregants thought would be around for a long time. But on May 31, 1917, a tornado leveled the church. Most agreed it was a miracle that the storm spared all three altars, the apse, façade, and steeple.

The same generation who built the second church would now be called to build a third church. The German farmers not only rebuilt the church, but built a much larger one, salvaging as much as possible from the old church. Designed by Dutch architect Frank A. Ludewig, Saint Peter's represented a brick German Romanesque basilica with byzantine touches; it was completed in one year.

Unlike other painted churches in Texas, the interior designs of Saint Peter's are more abstract and geometric, and more unified with the architectural forms. Swiss artist Friederich Fuchs painted the original folk art, which covered nearly every interior surface.

The commitment of the church members was tested yet again. In 2009, the beautiful painted plaster of the interior began to crumble. Careful inspection revealed roof damage, which had leaked water behind the interior plaster for years. Saint Peter's needed a major restoration. Led by Fort Worth architect Arthur Weinman, workers made structural repairs, and artists performed touch up or recreated the patterns and design on the interior, at a cost of $4.9 million.

Saint Peter's today stands strong and beautiful, a testimony of art and architecture and generations of committed care.

TEMPLE BETH-EL

CORSICANA
Built in 1900

It was the arrival of the Houston and Central Texas Railroad in 1871 that propelled Corsicana into a thriving economic center and also encouraged the arrival of more Jewish people to the area. The railroads provided an easy way to transport merchandise, which, in turn, encouraged the increase of Jewish merchants.

"The earliest Jews, who arrived with the conquistadors, came from Sephardic (Spanish-North African-Israeli) communities. After the Mexican period, Jewry in Texas was essentially populated by immigrants from Germany and Eastern Europe. The same broadsides that attracted their non-Jewish fellow immigrants from other countries and from other states attracted the Jews. Texas was a land of promise with seemingly limitless potential."[6] And Texas offered more religious freedom than Europe.

Temple Beth-El was organized by Reform Jews in Corsicana. A group of Orthodox Jews met in another building. Unlike other immigrant groups who built their churches first, Jewish settlers first purchased land and organized a cemetery, then benevolent societies, and finally the synagogue. An unknown architect designed Temple Beth-El in the Moorish Revival style, an architectural style first appearing in Germany in the mid-eighteen hundreds.

The specific design resembles a synagogue near Warsaw, Poland. Two other temples were also designed by the same architect—one in Charleston, West Virginia, and one in Butte, Montana. Temple Beth-El is a wood frame building, its large rose window sits over the main entrance flanked by two octagon towers. Onion-shaped domes covered with sheet metal top the towers. The "onion dome" is a dominant feature of Russian church architecture and was also popular for churches in Germany.

Dedicated in 1900, Temple Beth-El hosted a large public ceremony that included participation from Christian pastors, organ music, and singing of Psalms. The hosting rabbi paid tribute to the president of the Ladies Hebrew Benevolent Society, Carrie Freedman, saying, "Without her untiring efforts, there would have been no Jewish place of worship."[7]

Even though Corsicana continued to grow economically, the Reform Jewish population struggled to maintain its building and support a full-time rabbi. The discovery of oil in 1894 boosted growth for the Jewish mercantile class, but ultimately the "oil boom" provided Corsicana with a reputation as a rough frontier town, complete with thirty-five saloons. The passage of an alcohol prohibition law in 1900 impacted the city's Jews, many of whom owned saloons or liquor businesses.

The congregation disbanded in 1981 with the Temple Beth-El scheduled for demolition. The Navarro County Historical Society intervened and purchased the building in 1982. Local citizens organized a "Save the Temple Committee," and more than $100,000 was raised through state grants, dinners, musical reviews, and private donations to restore the building. Raiford Stripling, restoration architect, led the work. Today the Temple is used by the community for a variety of activities and club meetings.

The few remaining Jews in Corsicana, joined by others from surrounding communities, meet monthly in Temple Beth-El for services. Rabbi Frank Joseph, son of Ernest Joseph who served the Jewish community for more than thirty years, drives from Dallas to lead them. The Jewish heritage started long ago remains alive, as does the legacy of Temple Beth-El, standing today, witness to its religious roots and historical role.

CChristensen '15

McKenzie United Methodist Church

HONEY GROVE
Built in 1911
Architect: J. E. Flanders and J. J. Flanders

McKenzie United Methodist Church in Honey Grove stands today just as it was completed in 1911. The church was designed by John James Flanders and his cousin James Edward Flanders. James Edward Flanders was a well-known church architect in Texas, specializing mainly in Methodist churches. His characteristic towers identify a Flanders church.

But McKenzie exhibited a departure in style from Flanders's other churches. The 1911 church was actually a rebuilding of the older church built in 1881. Flanders used salvaged pressed red brick and rusticated stone for the new church's hexagonal towers and lower part of the building. In sharp contrast, white cast stone was used around the Gothic windows. Altar rails and pews were also from the earlier church but were eventually replaced.

Jacob Fein headed up construction. Fein constructed many of Honey Grove's buildings and worked as a stonemason on the Texas state capitol building. Limestone for McKenzie came from the nearby Floyd Quarry.

Methodism in the area can be traced to 1842 with a land donation and a one-room log cabin where congregants met. The church grew and moved in 1856 to Honey Grove, where it joined Union Church—a one-room log church shared by Baptists, Cumberland Presbyterians, and Methodists. The Methodists had the building for the fourth Sunday of every month.

It wasn't until 1879 that the Methodists pulled away from Union Church and began construction on their own building, named after Dr. J. W. P. McKenzie, a circuit rider who served the area and also ministered to the Choctaw Indians. Hosting the North Texas Annual Conference in 1887 provided the opportunity to expand the church.

Finally in 1910, with a growing congregation, construction on the current church began. Requests from the congregation included a domed ceiling, electrical chandelier, classrooms, and a space to house a pipe organ. The local newspaper, *Honey Grove Signal*, reported on Sunday morning, January 29, 1911, "The congregation entered the splendid new building cemented by the golden ties of love and determined to do great things for the extension of the Master's Kingdom on earth."

OUR MERCIFUL SAVIOUR EPISCOPAL CHURCH

KAUFMAN
Built in 1909
Architect: Walter Slack

Tucked on a street corner in Kaufman stands an unassuming frame church—simple lines, a green exterior merging into the surrounding grass and gardens, and a red door inviting entry. Our Merciful Saviour Episcopal Church, the little green church, stands as an enduring testimony to the love of one man for his wife, and the love of a congregation for their savior.

Our Merciful Saviour was organized as a mission in 1883. Built in 1909, the rural Gothic church construction was led by Woodson Nash. Nash had married an Episcopalian from Galveston, Cecile Noble. When Cecile became homesick, Woodson asked what she missed most about Galveston. She missed the Gulf and her Episcopal church. Woodson acknowledged he could do nothing about the Gulf, but certainly he could provide the church.

Woodson obtained plans from a friend who had built an Episcopal church in nearby Forney. The original plans were designed by an Episcopalian architect, Walter Slack of New Bedford, Massachusetts. Today the little green church still welcomes people to worship. The ceiling, walls, and pews are all the original wood, and the stained-glass windows are as they were built in 1909. The original cross for the top of the church is preserved behind glass in the church foyer.

"It's old, but it isn't a museum," are the opening words of a 2006 article in *The Kaufman Herald* celebrating the church's long-standing existence. "That is the message members of Episcopal Church of Our Merciful Saviour in Kaufman want people to know—their little green church is not a museum—it is an active church holding weekly services and other activities."[8]

CJC
CJChristensen 15

4

Historic Churches of South Central Texas

1. WESTPHALIA
   CHURCH OF THE VISITATION
2. WESLEY
   WESLEY BRETHREN
3. INDEPENDENCE
   INDEPENDENCE BAPTIST
4. INDEPENDENCE
   LIBERTY BAPTIST
5. LAGRANGE
   ST. JAMES EPISCOPAL
6. LOCKHART
   FIRST CHRISTIAN
7. LOCKHART
   EMMANUEL EPISCOPAL
8. PRAHA
   ST. MARY'S CATHOLIC
9. DUBINA
   STS. CYRIL AND METHODIUS CATHOLIC
10. PLANTERSVILLE
    ST. MARY'S CATHOLIC
11. SERBIN
    ST. PAUL'S LUTHERAN

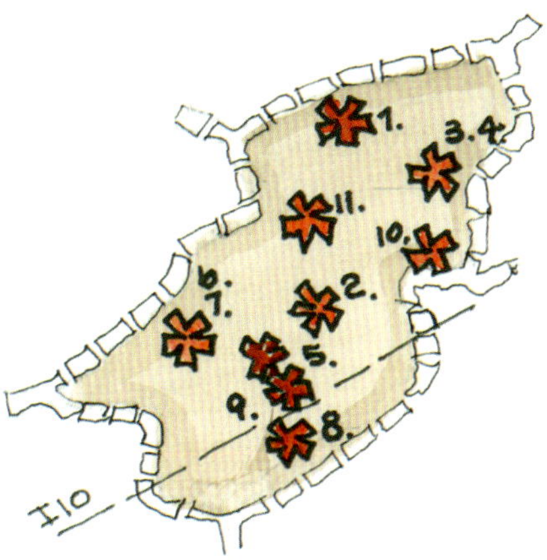

CHURCH OF THE VISITATION

WESTPHALIA
Built in 1895
Architect: Rev. H. M. Simoni

The sturdy German settlers, looking for good soil to farm, learned from the hard lessons Texas weather dished out. They named their community Westphalia after their home province in Germany. Ten acres of land were quickly purchased for a school and church. But both of those first structures, completed in 1884, were destroyed by a storm in May 1885.

Undaunted in their determination to establish a church, the community supported the Reverend P. M. Simoni as he drew up the plans for a building in the shape of a Latin cross. Parishioners hired Andrews Fuchs of Waco to lead the volunteer construction team.

All materials—stone from a quarry in Muldoon and timber from Waco—were hauled by the locals from Lott, eight miles away, where the railroad delivered them.

With the storm experience still vivid in their memories, six inches of "sway" were built into the two bell towers, to protect the church from future windstorms. Topped with copper sheeting, each tower held a nine-foot stainless steel cross at the top, with a six-foot cross in the center.

Twenty stained-glass windows were shipped from Germany. The church's "namesake" window, installed behind the main altar, is the largest window and depicts the visitation of the Virgin Mary.

The Church of the Visitation, one of the largest wooden churches in Texas, was recognized with a Texas historical marker in December 1978 and still serves as the focal point of the community. The area farmland, which first drew the German settlers, received recognition in 1996 as a Rural Historic District.

Wesley Brethren Church

Wesley
Built in 1866

The simplicity of the white frame church building gives no hint of the intricate paintings and rich history behind the door. Wesley Brethren Church housed the first congregation in Texas of the Czech-Moravian Brethren. The Protestant Czechs immigrated to Texas in the 1850s and named their settlement *Veseli* (Wesley), which means happy or joyous. Built in 1866 of oak logs and local stone, the church building served as a school until about 1900.

The Reverend Bohuslav Laciak, a Czech immigrant pastor and teacher, painted the interior of the church in 1889. Descendants of early church members tell stories of Laciak on a ladder painting the ceiling while the children were doing their schoolwork. The pastor, who spoke Czech and German, devoted three years to the church artwork. Before he could complete all that he had planned to paint, he was killed in a hunting accident.

Laciak's artwork has met with ongoing debate on why he painted certain things. Most agree that painting columns and archways on the side walls provided a basilica-style look for the little building. It is thought that the painted brick walls represented the walls of old Jerusalem or implied a meaning of protection for believers within the walls of the church building.

Above the pulpit, the painted gold chalice symbolizes the blood of Christ. The ceiling, painted blue with bright-gold geometric patterns, probably represents heaven. The color blue in Czechoslovakian culture represents God. The Czechoslovakian phrase over the outside door translates: "I am the way, the truth and the life."

Inside the church, the original German pump organ still stands in the corner, and the original church bell still rings out for congregants. Also, the original Bibles with a chalice design on the front cover are still in the church. Freedom to read the Word of God is a core value for the Brethren, whose roots trace back to the priest John Hus. Hus believed scriptures should be provided to people in their language instead of the Latin version, which only the clergy or highly educated had the opportunity to read.

cjc
Carl Christensen '14

INDEPENDENCE BAPTIST CHURCH

INDEPENDENCE
Built in 1872

Independence Baptist Church holds the title of the oldest, continuously active Baptist church in Texas. Organized in August 1839 by the Reverend Thomas Spraggins and a small group of Baptists, the total membership that year grew to fifteen. Independence Baptist was a strong supporter of missionary work during the Republic of Texas.

The church had strong ties to Baylor University, also located in Independence from 1846–86. The church's pastor was often the president of the university, and the church shared facilities with the university. The church members voted to construct a new building in 1858 on land donated by Rufus Burleson, Baylor president and church pastor. The building, with one-foot-thick walls, was severely damaged by fire in 1872. Congregants rebuilt the same year with some of the original walls that had survived.

One well-known leader from the Texas Revolution, Sam Houston, was baptized at the church on November 19, 1854. Sam Houston's pew, which also survived the fire of 1872, is marked for visitors today.

Prior to the Civil War, separate services were offered for the slaves of church members. In 1866, the African American members established their own church, Liberty Baptist Church. Today, Independence Baptist is a growing congregation, cognizant of its heritage both in Texas history and denominational history. A new facility serves the congregation, but special services are still held in the historic sanctuary.

Carl Christensen '12
Independence Baptist Church

LIBERTY BAPTIST CHURCH

INDEPENDENCE
Built in 1900

In the South following the Civil War, a mass movement occurred of African Americans leaving white-controlled churches to establish their own churches. Such was the case with the congregation of Liberty Baptist, made up of African Americans who had strong ties with Independence Baptist Church. In 1871, more than 150 African Americans united to form their new Baptist church.

Services were held in a variety of places, and the exact date when the first church building was established is not known. A notice in the local paper in September 1879 indicates that lumber was purchased for a new church. Another article in February 1882 reported that a storm had blown through and blown the church down.

The 1900 cornerstone of the current church may indicate the new building's date after suffering damage from another storm in September 1900. The original shape of the sanctuary is still clear: a cruciform configuration, gabled entry, and center steeple.

Several years after the building of the 1900 church, a school for African American children in the area was established next to Liberty Baptist. African American churches played a key role in educating children and adults during that time period in Texas history.

Liberty Baptist today bears witness to the religious and cultural history of the African American community in Independence.

Carl Christensen '12

SAINT JAMES EPISCOPAL CHURCH

LA GRANGE
1855–56
Architect: Richard M. Upjohn

The story of Saint James Church in La Grange lies in its tenacity of spirit and its perseverance in times of adversity. Through the years, the challenges have included a yellow fever epidemic that killed half of the church membership, devastating floods on the Colorado River, and changing population demographics. With every adversity, the commitment, love, and hard work of key people kept the vision for Saint James alive.

Two of the key people in the life of Saint James were Judge and Mrs. Benjamin Shropshire, who joined the small congregation in 1852. In 1858 Benjamin Shropshire attended a diocesan convention, where he passionately presented the need for the diocese to send a full-time rector to La Grange. The judge fell victim to the yellow fever epidemic and died in 1867. To honor his love for the church, Mrs. Shropshire donated land for the church building and worked to secure financial support for the building.

Another key figure in Saint James history was the Reverend William George Washington, who was installed as rector in 1881. Reverend Washington made numerous fundraising trips to New York and oversaw plans for the new church. He also arranged for the transfer of the church land back to the Shropshire heirs, in exchange for the lot on which the current church stands. Reverend Washington also designed and built the altar, lectern, communion rail, bishop's chair, and pews—all of which are still in use today.

The church building opened in 1885, with a memorial window presented by the children of the late Judge and Mrs. Shropshire. As a testament to the hardships endured over the years, the stained glass called "Faith" was commissioned. Made by a well-known European artist, the window was shipped on the Steamship *City of Berlin*. The ship struck an iceberg en route, but miraculously, despite extensive damage to the ship's upper plates and deck, and tons of ice smashing into the ship's hold, the precious glass was not damaged.

Saint James is a model of Queen Anne style, an architectural revival in England that arrived in the United States in the 1870s. Shingles cover most of the walls and pitched roof. Louvered, screened openings, closed by interior removable panels, allowed for air circulation in the hot weather. Wood trusses supporting the roof over the altar area were, according to church history, "inspired by the hulls of ships sailing the Sea of Galilee in the days of Christ's earthly ministry."

For a period of twenty years in the early 1900s, the congregation was small enough that a full-time rector was not needed. The church stood vacant. The grounds were overgrown with wild grass. The sanctuary floor was neglected and dirty; the windows and door locks were broken. According to a *Houston Daily Post* article, bats resided in the belfry. But when a rector was once again assigned to La Grange, the church was cleaned up and has remained open to this day, witness to the commitment and faith of both the founding members and today's congregation.

cjchristensen '14

cjchristensen '15

FIRST CHRISTIAN CHURCH

LOCKHART
Built in 1898
Architect: Tom Hodges

"Like many historical churches, First Christian Church began in 1852 not with a building but a belief, and members met in a Masonic Hall."[1] Seven members met to start First Christian. The first sanctuary was constructed in 1858, and the church membership soon outgrew the facility.

Architect Tom Hodges, who designed Lockhart's courthouse, town jail, and library, designed the Gothic Revival church building in 1898. The building exhibits classic Gothic Revival elements: lancet windows, decorative brickwork, corner turrets with stone, and arched doorways.

In the early days of the church, a stock tank outside served as the baptistery. Whenever a baptism was scheduled, firemen from the Lockhart Volunteer Hook and Ladder Company, as it was called then, took their fire hoses and filled the tank with water. The relationship between the firefighters and church members has grown over the years. Today the church honors the firefighters yearly during Firefighter Appreciation Week and continues to serve food and fellowship whenever the firefighters visit.

First Christian, one block off of downtown, takes up nearly an entire block with its beautiful, powerful presence.

cjchristensen'14

EMMANUEL EPISCOPAL CHURCH

LOCKHART
Built in 1856

Emmanuel Episcopal Church in Lockhart might summon adjectives of quaint, charming, and cozy. None of those would aptly describe the bold construction and the historic title this church holds.

Church founder Rev. Joseph Wood Dunn is credited with organizing the church's construction. Arriving in Lockhart in August 1853, Dunn held the first church service in a school. A year later when he was told the school was no longer available for services, he started funds to build.

Four Lockhart residents agreed to build the roof and install windows if Dunn would be responsible for the walls. Dunn ordered the construction of two-foot-thick walls, extending two feet underground. Ceiling beams were hand-hewn cedar timbers, and local limestone formed the floor. Window frames, chancery rails, and the altar were all built of hand-carved native walnut.

Completed in 1856, Emmanuel Episcopal holds the title of "oldest known unaltered church building in use by Protestants in Texas."[2] A restoration project in 1976 returned the church to its original form, including refinished limestone slabs on the floor. Today, visitors can view Dunn's Bible and Prayer Book on display—testimony to Dunn's determination and vision for the little Lockhart church.

CJChristensen-'15

SAINT MARY'S CHURCH

PRAHA
Built in 1895
Architect: O. Kramer

The painted churches of Texas reveal the passion of nineteenth-century immigrants who left behind European culture, customs, and centuries of treasured art and architecture to live on untamed frontier land. The churches' exterior facades do not hint of the visual feast of design, color, and imagery adorning every interior surface with murals and designs.

Saint Mary's Church of the Assumption, built in 1891, is one of the oldest of the painted churches. Bohemian immigrant Mathias Novak arrived in the area, originally called Mulberry, in the mid-1850s. Novak bought land and built a frame house to celebrate early masses. As more Czech immigrants arrived, the town was renamed Praha in honor of the immigrants' home, Prague.

The first Catholic church in Praha was built of wood in 1868. In 1875 a new church was built; the present rock building was completed in 1895. Dedication services drew ten thousand people, mostly Germans and Bohemians. The article in the *Weimar Mercury* on November 30, 1895, described it as "the scene of the grandest affair in its (Praha's) history." Following the dedication, the priest delivered three sermons, one in German, one in Bohemian, and one in English.

"Local history says that a keg of beer was offered to the man who dared top the church steeple with a cross," recounted Alan Oakes in an article accompanying the 2001 KLRU documentary film, *The Painted Churches of Texas: Echoes of the Homeland.* "At over 130 feet, climbing to the top was no doubt a harrowing feat. Evidently a man who put crosses on steeples for a living took the community up on their offer. After he bravely affixed the cross to the top of the steeple the man proceeded to do a handstand on top of the cross."

Swiss-born artist Gottfried Flury from Moulton, Texas, painted much of Saint Mary's interior. Flury mixed his own paints and adorned the ceiling and walls with rich turquoise and green hues, and images of ferns, flowers, and angels. In 1901, Saint Mary's priest, Father Netardus, added more interior designs. Gene A. Mikulik, who took care of several churches in the area, including Saint Mary's, restored much of the sanctuary art, adding gold leafing and new paint to the altars.

Since 1855, parish members and visitors have celebrated the Feast of Assumption of the Blessed Virgin Mary, the church's namesake. This church picnic, called the Prazska Pout or Praha Picnic, is held annually on August 15 and draws as many as five thousand visitors.

cjchristensen '14

SAINTS CYRIL AND METHODIUS CATHOLIC CHURCH

DUBINA
Built in 1912
Architect: Leo Dielmann

As if the fourteen-week, cross-Atlantic trip followed by a ferry ride up Buffalo Bayou and then a five-day ox-cart ride wasn't enough to discourage the settlers from Moravia, certainly when they reached their destination that night in November 1856, sleeping under an oak grove while enduring a Texas sleet storm should have been.

Judge August Haidusek later recalled the Texas arrival, which he experienced at age twelve: "It was raining and sleeting when we arrived by wagon at a spot studded with oaks. Here, soaked with the rain, we were left at the mercy of the weather; the only protection was the branches of the spreading oaks."

But these Czech settlers endured and moved forward with their hardy spirit and strong faith. The Texas Historical Commission has designated Dubina, which means oak grove in Czech, as the first Czech settlement in Texas. Other Czechs had arrived and settled in the state, but this group marked the first settlement solely comprised of Czechs.

The Dubina Catholic colonists first met as a church in a log cabin in May 1857. A priest traveled to Dubina to serve communion three to four times a year. Many would walk for a day and spend the night outside the cabin in order to celebrate mass.

After several years of fundraising, the first church building was completed in 1877. A freed slave, Tom Lee, made an iron cross to top the steeple.

A hurricane that hit the Texas coast in 1909 destroyed the church building. Undaunted, the settlers hired prominent Texas architect Leo Dielmann and started rebuilding that very year. Completed in 1912, the interior of the church was covered with frescos and stenciled designs. In 1952, for whatever reason, the interior of the church was whitewashed, hiding all the beautiful designs.

Judge Ed Janecka, who once served as an altar boy in the church, recalled seeing faint traces of earlier designs when sunlight hit the walls. It was Judge Janecka and Butch Koenig who led a restoration of the interior in the 1980s. Local artists uncovered old designs, and the original stencils were found and used to fill in the vines, oak leaves, and angels on the sky-blue ceiling and walls. The judge himself painted the last angel to the left of the choir loft.

Today, of all the painted churches in Texas, Saints Cyril and Methodius Church is called "the grandest lady of them all."

CJchristensen '14

SAINT MARY'S CATHOLIC CHURCH

PLANTERSVILLE
Built in 1917

Seventy families comprised the first Catholic parish in Plantersville in 1894. Catholic priests had visited Plantersville for the first time in 1860, and the Catholics met in the home of James Kelly Markey until 1873 when the first building was constructed.

In the last part of the nineteenth century, so many German-Russian and Polish immigrants began to arrive in Plantersville that a full-time priest was assigned to the growing parish. Ten acres of donated land and the hard work of the parishioners helped create the small building dedicated in 1894 with the name Nativity of the Blessed Virgin Mary.

In 1907, the Polish and German congregants within the church split; the Polish Catholics formed a church in nearby Stoneham. Saint Mary's continued to grow, making improvements to the building until July 1917 when lightning struck the church and it was completely destroyed by fire. The current Saint Mary's was rebuilt that same year, debt free.

The Gothic Revival church includes the typical lancet windows, buttresses, and bell tower of that style of architecture. The stained-glass windows depict the parishioners' German heritage.

SAINT PAUL LUTHERAN CHURCH

SERBIN
Built in 1871

From the exterior, Saint Paul Lutheran Church in Serbin looks plain, almost austere. On the inside, it's another story, and the beautiful display of color proves why Saint Paul is recognized as one of Texas' painted churches.

Wendish immigrants from Lusatia, an area in eastern Germany, founded the church in 1854. Rev. Jan Kilian led a group of 500 Wendish to Texas from Hamburg, Germany, the one mass exodus of Wends from their home country. The Wends wanted two things: religious freedom and cheap, plentiful land. Texas provided both.

On the first leg of their trip, sailing to Liverpool, many contracted cholera. Seventy-three Wends died. A yellow fever epidemic greeted their arrival in Galveston. From the coast, the Wends walked more than eighty miles to the land purchased for them in Lee County and established the community of Serbin.

Kilian's two-room house provided a place for church services until the settlers could build. Saint Paul, the first Missouri Synod Lutheran Church in Texas, was built in 1871.

The dominant feature of the interior is the pulpit, the tallest pulpit in Texas, located on the upper level of the church. The upper-level balcony lines both sides of the church and is reserved for men and boys. The women and children sit downstairs. Traditional separation of the men from women in churches dates back to AD 300. The Wendish church follows the tradition but reverses the location, seating the women and children on the main level instead of the balcony.

Today the Texas Wendish Heritage Museum in Serbin depicts the heritage and history of the Wendish immigrants and their culture. Visitors can tour Saint Paul in addition to exhibits in several other buildings.

Carl Christensen '15

5

Historic Churches of the Hill Country

1. MASON
HILDA BETHEL ME

2. FREDRICKSBURG
ST. MARY'S CATHOLIC

3. FREDRICKSBURG
ZION LUTHERAN

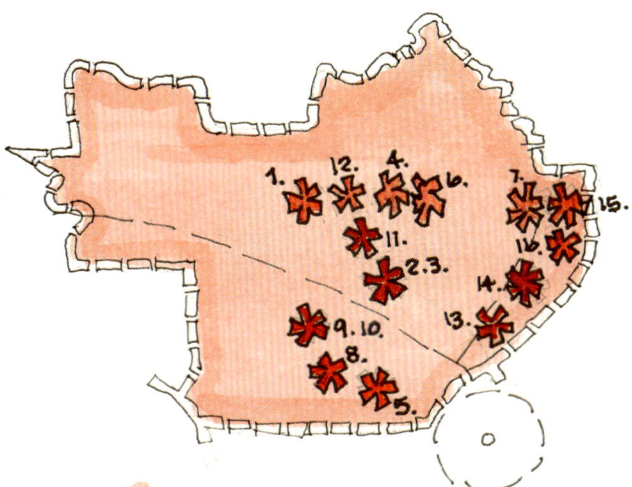

15. BARTLETT
FIRST UNITED METHODIST

16. GEORGETOWN
WESLEY CHAPEL AME

4. CASTELL
TRINITY UNITED METHODIST

5. CASTROVILLE
ST. LOUIS CATHOLIC

6. LLANO
GRACE EPISCOPAL

7. NEW SWEDEN
EVANGELICAL LUTHERAN

8. QUIHI
BETHLEHEM LUTHERAN

9. BANDERA
ST. STANISLAUS CATHOLIC

10. BANDERA
POLLY'S CHAPEL

11. GRABAPPLE
ST. JOHN'S LUTHERAN

12. ART
ART UNITED METHODIST

13. SAN MARCOS
FIRST UNITED METHODIST

14. NEW BRAUNFELS
STS. PETER AND PAUL CATHOLIC

HILDA UNITED METHODIST CHURCH

MASON
Built in 1902

In the 1800s, Hilda, formerly known as the community of Beaver Creek, was on the edge of the frontier. Native American tribes frequently raided the small community named by the first postmistress, Emma Schulze. Supplies were short and required travel to Fredericksburg, thirty-five miles away. But the German immigrants, part of the "overflow" from Fredericksburg and New Braunfels, were not to be deterred. While most of these early German immigrants identified with the Lutheran and Catholic churches, the small group that settled Hilda was devout Methodists.

Built in 1902, the First Methodist Church replaced the original church from 1862 and recycled stones from the original building. Richard Grosse, a lumberyard owner from Mason, designed the church. As it turned out, Grosse was an extraordinarily skilled German stonemason who crafted Hilda's church and the Lutheran church in Mason.

The first church built in 1865 served as school and church. *Ess hauzen*, or eating houses, were added on the fifty-acre property as a place for church members and families. Travel to Sunday services was by horseback, wagon, or on foot; the *ess hauzen* served as a place for families to eat meals Sunday evenings or stay overnight if needed. With the introduction of automobiles in the 1930s, the *ess hauzen* fell into disuse; only two remain today. The only language spoken in church was German.

Today, Hilda is a ghost town with little remaining except a truly magnificent Methodist church.

SAINT MARY'S CATHOLIC CHURCH

FREDERICKSBURG
Built in 1908
Architect: Leo Dielmann

Deeply rooted in Fredericksburg's German history, Saint Mary's Catholic Church is the evolution of three separate church buildings. The Catholics forming Saint Mary's first met in Fredericksburg's public building, *Vereins-Kirche*, which served as the first school, town hall, and place of worship for all religious groups.

The Catholic worshippers were the first to build their own church—a log-house style building—in 1848. The church body grew, and in 1860 Saint Mary's Church, *Marienkirche*, was built. The building exemplified strong Gothic features: pointed arch windows, stone buttresses, and a distinctive steeple, with a pristine, almost austere interior. Again, growth outmatched the facilities, and the third and present-day church that some parishioners still refer to as the "new" church, was built. Started in 1905 and completed in 1908, the church was designed by Leo Dielmann, an architect from San Antonio, and built of local quarried stone.

The pipe organ, installed in 1906, was one of only three such organs in the state of Texas. Sanctuary windows were also installed in 1906. Two stained-glass windows, depicting a boy and a girl with their guardian angels, were made in Germany. The boy, James Blum, died in 1905 at age six from an infection that developed into spinal meningitis. The girl in the window, Erna Wagner, daughter of Jacob Wagner, the contractor of Saint Mary's, died at age five of diphtheria.

The rest of more than twelve magnificent stained-glass windows were installed in 1914–15. Saint Mary's also houses numerous statues and paintings of Catholic saints and specific events in the life of Christ.

Stations of the cross were installed before the church was completed, and the German wording remained until 1936. At that time, the first major refurbishing of the church was accomplished and all the stenciling and art work done. Moisture seeping through the rock walls drove another renovation in 1970, and efforts were made to retain as much of the original artwork as possible. With paintings and murals throughout the interior, including the ceiling vaults and organ pipes, Saint Mary's is recognized as one of Texas' painted churches.

Architecturally, Saint Mary's features trefoil motifs, a corner tower, and stone buttresses.

A legend behind the stones of Saint Mary's describes a stranger who visited the men gathering and cutting the stones in the hot Texas sun. The stranger questioned three of the workers, asking each the same question, "*Was tuest Du?*" ("What are you doing?"). The first answered, "Oh, I have to haul these darn rocks." The second replied, "I don't think I'll ever get finished cutting these rocks for this huge building." But the third man responded differently, "I'm building a cathedral for the glory of God!" Legend suggests the stranger was Christ himself, who blessed the third stonecutter and then disappeared.[1]

cjchristensen 14

cjchristensen 14

ZION LUTHERAN CHURCH

FREDERICKSBURG
Built in 1854

With luminarias lining the walkway, white lights outlining the building, and a simple, bright star adorning the top, Zion Lutheran Church glows bright and brilliant during the Advent season. The tradition of luminarias originated in Spain, where people lit bonfires along roadsides and churchyards to lead the way to midnight Mass or to commemorate the journey of the Holy Family. The tradition found its way to Mexico, then to Spanish villages along the Rio Grande, and then to Texas settlements including Fredericksburg.

Six German families organized Zion, the Hill Country's first Lutheran church, in 1852. They originally worshipped with other church groups, including Catholics and Methodists at the *Vereins-Kirche*, the first public building in Fredericksburg. All religious groups met in the building until, one by one, they built their own facilities.

These founding Zion Church members helped build the sanctuary of native limestone, completing it in 1854. A stucco-over-stone wall, built in 1878, protected the church from animals, mostly cattle, roaming up and down Main Street.

An enlarged sanctuary, new chancel area, and bell tower—all added in 1908—accommodated congregational growth for Zion. Three bronze bells, installed in 1963, replaced the original single cast-iron bell.

Zion stands tall and proud today, anchoring one end of Fredericksburg's Main Street, serving the community with social and spiritual programs, and still lighting the way to Advent celebrations.

CK Christensen '14

TRINITY UNITED METHODIST CHURCH

CASTELL

Built in 1880

The story of Castell's historic Methodist church started with a Methodist circuit rider, willing to brave the elements and dangers of frontier life to serve people. The Reverend Charles A. Grote, assigned to the Methodist Episcopal Church South in Fredericksburg, often traveled by horseback to the Llano River Valley to minister to German settlers in the area. Grote ultimately organized the Llano Valley Circuit, serving the German Methodists as a circuit rider.

On one of his rides, Grote faced down three heavy thunderstorms, no small feat. He then arrived at the south bank of the Llano River at Castell to find the stream at flood stage. The next morning, churchgoers on the north bank saw the reverend stuck and sent Native Americans to bring him across on horseback.

The Native Americans wanted him to ride the horse across the water, but Grote, unable to swim, preferred to hold onto the horse's tail and kick his feet. Two Native Americans swam alongside him; a third swam in front of the horse. By the time they reached an island close to the north shore, Grote had swallowed so much water, he nearly drowned. Instead of continuing on that way, the rescuers stretched a rope to a tree on the north bank and helped pull him to shore.

As the story goes, Grote immediately changed clothes and preached with fervor under a large live oak. Before he finished, the people fell to their knees in prayer at this first public worship service on the Llano River. As many more Germans from Fredericksburg began to settle in the area, Grote was appointed full-time pastor to the Methodist church in Castell in 1871, and the congregation built a church with a parsonage.

In 1880 the first section of the Castell church was built, a simple wood-frame structure with arched windows on the sides. The bell for the church was purchased and placed in the bell tower in 1891.

Merging with Hoersterville Methodist Episcopal Church in 1939, the church changed its name to Trinity Methodist Church. Hoersterville's church building was torn down and reassembled as a fellowship hall and education building next to the Castell church.

Trinity United marked its one 160th year of services in 2012 with a building renovation. People can still worship on Sundays at Trinity in Castell, the "oldest surviving settlement in Llano County."

Carl Christensen '12

SAINT LOUIS CATHOLIC CHURCH

CASTROVILLE
Built in 1870
Architect: Reverend Richard Peter

Following in the tradition of French colonial communities, Saint Louis Catholic Church in Castroville opens to a central, public community space. In communities like this, a church's location reflected "the hierarchical importance of religion to Texas societies," wrote Willard Robinson in *Reflections of Faith, Houses of Worship in the Lone Star State.*

Castroville was founded by Henri Castro, an empresario who brought settlers from the Alsace-Lorraine area of France in September 1844. Just one week later, Jean Marie Odin, a French priest who would soon become the first Catholic bishop of Texas, celebrated mass on the Medina River banks. Father Odin also placed the cornerstone of what would be the settlement's first Catholic church.

The first church was completed in 1846 and now stands, restored, nearly a block from the current Saint Louis. On Easter Sunday, 1850, the second church was dedicated. The plans to build the third and current church greeted a young French priest assigned to Castroville. He knew the structure wouldn't be large enough, so he offered to help finance the building if the parishioners agreed to follow his design.

The Reverend Richard Peter drew up plans for the church: a basilican design with a clearly defined nave and side aisles. Built of limestone and cypress, the current church spire reaches 110 feet skyward. Painted reredos and decorative work represent the French Gothic tradition.

Saint Louis was completed on August 25, 1870, the day of the feast of Saint Louis. Since that time, Saint Louis Day has been celebrated yearly, growing to become one of the largest church celebrations in Texas. Today Saint Louis feast day is celebrated on the Sunday nearest August 25, drawing thousands to Castroville.

Carl Christensen '14

GRACE EPISCOPAL CHURCH

LLANO
Built in 1890

In 1859, fourteen years before Llano County's last Native American fight—a skirmish known as the Packsaddle Mountain Fight—one faithful couple had observed daily services for three years from the Episcopalian Book of Common Prayer. Unknown to them, they had established the roots of what would become Grace Episcopal Church.

Llano was just one place assigned to the bishop of the West Texas diocese, covering the area from Brownsville to El Paso. Because Llano was considered so challenging and dangerous, the bishop often required an army escort to visit the town's few Episcopalian faithful. Formal services started in the early 1880s.

It took another couple, W. L. Johnson and his wife, Ida, to set in motion the provision of a building. The Johnsons came to Llano to start a school, persuading the city commissioners to allocate land for the building of a school. Construction began—a simple, sturdy building of native stone, but before construction could be completed, the school program failed. Johnson sold the land and unfinished building for $300.

Two years later, the building and property came into the hands of the bishop of the West Texas Missionary District of the Episcopal Church and the Standing Committee of Grace Church, Llano. Much work had to be done; the building needed walls, windows, a roof, and a floor—a daunting challenge for a church of only seven or eight people and very little money.

The discovery of iron ore in the late 1880s propelled population growth and the urgency to complete the building. Finally on April 17, 1890, the first service and communion celebration was held in the church building, which was still not fully completed. The bishop wrote: "Preached and celebrated Holy Communion in the church at Llano. It was the first service I had in the Church which, by the indefatigable efforts of the members, had been floored since my last visit."[2]

Today the church looks as it did in the 1890s—a sturdy oblong box with arched windows and front door—a secure haven in the surrounding landscape of live oaks and a solid testimony to years of commitment and faithful giving to complete the church.

Carl Christensen '10

NEW SWEDEN EVANGELICAL LUTHERAN CHURCH

NEW SWEDEN
Built in 1923

Pastor Hans Lilleford of New Sweden Evangelical Lutheran Church calls the church the "most photographed church in Texas." Certainly the church is a notable landmark of Travis County. Its 104-foot copper steeple can be seen for miles in the rolling hills and pasture land surrounding the church.

New Sweden began with forty-three Swedish immigrants: twenty-seven men, sixteen women, and twenty-four children. The first church, completed in 1879, housed a steadily growing congregation. People traveled to church on foot, by horseback, wagon, and buggy over dirt and mud roads.

Construction started on the existing New Sweden church in 1921 and was completed two years later. Today the congregation is a blend of direct descendants of the original Swedish immigrants and new arrivals to the community. The church still observes several Swedish traditions, including Easter Sunday morning service at the local cemetery and early Christmas morning *Julatta*—a service that celebrates the time of birth of Jesus and where Swedish songs are still heard today.

CJC
CJChristensen'14

BETHLEHEM LUTHERAN CHURCH

QUIHI
Built in 1914

Quihi is a ghost town, but it was once a thriving community of French settlers thanks to Frenchman Henri Castro. Castro became an American citizen and land entrepreneur after he was appointed French consul at Providence, Rhode Island. In 1842, Texas Republic President Sam Houston offered Castro a land grant, promising him more than a million acres of land if he would bring at least six hundred families and/or single men and establish four towns. For the colonists to receive 640 acres, each family had to build a cabin, cultivate the land, and live there for three years.

Castro energetically recruited settlers, mostly from the Alsace area of France. Eventually Castro's recruitment efforts to Texas were second only to Stephen F. Austin. The first settlement for the Alsace immigrants became Castroville, followed shortly by Quihi.

The first ten families moved to Quihi in 1846. Native Americans killed two families soon after they arrived, and tribes continued to plague the settlers up until the 1870s.

With the help of the minister from Castroville's Lutheran church, Quihi's Bethlehem Lutheran Church was formed in 1852. Parishioners helped build the present church in 1914. Bethlehem Lutheran, still an active church, is one of the few remaining structures in Quihi.

CJC
CJChristensen '14

POLLY'S CHAPEL

BANDERA
Built in 1882
Architect: José Policarpio "Polly" Rodriquez

Polly's Chapel, located about sixteen miles outside of Bandera, celebrates one man's faith and commitment to the land and community where he lived.

José Policarpio "Polly" Rodriquez, one of the first settlers of San Antonio and Bandera, moved from Mexico to San Antonio when he was twelve. The young boy apprenticed to a gun maker, then worked as a guide and surveyor for US Army officers. Polly bought 360 acres of land on Privilege Creek in 1858 for fifty cents an acre.

Over the years he distinguished himself as a Native American fighter, rancher, scout, and Texas Ranger, eventually accumulating four thousand acres of the land he loved. Polly seemed to excel at whatever he did. It was said he trained his horse to deer hunt like a dog.

His accomplishments provided him the opportunity to sell homesteading land to relatives and other settlers. He also developed the small town named after him.

Through testimonials from his cousin, he converted to the Methodist faith, causing a rift with some of his family and neighbors. Pursuing his newfound faith, Polly turned to preaching as a circuit rider. He thought the town of Polly, where he had donated land for a school and post office, needed a church, so he built the chapel by hand in 1882.

Polly's Chapel is a simple, one-story, rectangular building of native stone that can seat up to one hundred people. Finding this unique building of Texas history continues to challenge visitors. Polly chose a site off of Privilege Creek Road, tucked back in the woods on a small rise facing the creek and taking advantage of southwestern breezes.

Today, his great grandson oversees the chapel, which is owned by the Methodist Episcopal Church. Visitors from forty-eight states and fourteen foreign countries visited Polly's Chapel from 2006 to 2008. The man who left his mark on this countryside is buried in the cemetery near the chapel. His tombstone reads, "By nature strong, fearless, and daring; by grace, an apostle to his people winning many souls to Christ. He suffered privation, persecution, sorrow, unmoved he went with joy and singing to the end."

SAINT STANISLAUS CATHOLIC CHURCH

BANDERA
Built in 1876

When the Polish Silesians arrived in San Antonio in December 1854, Father Leopold Moczygemba guided them to the place he had selected, now known as Panna Maria. However, the settlers heard news about Bandera, which had a sawmill and jobs. The rumors flew: Bandera was beautiful, with similar features to their Polish homeland, and abundant, free water (water in Panna Maria cost twenty-five cents a barrel). Eleven families chose Bandera.

In 1859, the group built a log structure, measuring 20 feet by 30 feet, to serve as their first church. For one dollar, the settlers purchased the entire block of land. By 1874 the settlers needed to build a stone convent to house the nuns who taught school to the settlers' children. The current church, built of native limestone, was constructed in 1876. Various alterations occurred over the next one hundred years, including the completion of a steeple and the addition of stained-glass windows, a baptistery, confessionals, and a stainless steel cross.

An interior refurbishing started in Saint Stanislaus's centennial year, 1976. Over the next twenty-seven years, the church added six new stained-glass windows, cleaned the exterior limestone, and refurbished the marble on all the altars. The church also rewired its electrical system and added new air conditioning and heating.

Most important, the interior was transformed with new painted designs, including the symbols of the four evangelists on the ceiling, and murals on the walls and entrance. Saint Stanislaus, second oldest Polish church in the United States, stands proud and tall, its towered steeple overseeing the stone convent, which is now a museum, and the original rectory, built in 1897.

©c christensen'14

SAINT JOHN LUTHERAN CHURCH

CRABAPPLE
Built in 1897

Only three structures remain in the ghost town that was once the community of Crabapple: the Crabapple School, Saint John's Lutheran Church, and a brush arbor. The history of the church is intricately woven from the other two.

A group of Germans settled in Crabapple in the mid-eighteen hundreds. The school was established by 1867. Families living in Crabapple attended Zion Lutheran Church of Fredericksburg, but traveling the twenty or so miles became more difficult and grew to be unacceptable to these pioneers. They began to meet in the home of Mathias Schmidt, one of Crabapple's founders.

The building of a school in 1877 provided a place for the home church to meet and to secure a full-time pastor. In 1885 a larger school building allowed more room for church services. Social gatherings often took place at the brush arbor.

Finally in 1890, the church group joined the American Lutheran Church Synod of Texas and became a formal organization: Saint Johannes Evangelische Lutherische Kirche zu Crabapple, Texas. Six acres of land were purchased for a church building, which was finally completed in 1897.

Saint John's Lutheran models "vernacular architecture"—architecture based on local needs and construction materials. For the Crabapple church, this meant native limestone and masonry. Congregants entered the church through double doors, and in the winter were warmed by a wood-burning stove standing in the middle of the church.

Worship services stopped in 1962, but Saint John's still hosts yearly homecoming services on the fourth Sunday in September, weddings, and other family events. Visitors today find Saint John's down a country lane, simple and stately, silent with its treasury of memories, timeless in its service to the community.

Carl Christensen '14

ART UNITED METHODIST CHURCH

ART
Built in 1890
Architect: Richard Grosse

Art United Methodist Church is "one of the finest examples of the German settlers' churches" built in the last quarter of the nineteenth century. It represents the solid stone construction characteristic of German Texas settlements and was built by German Texas stonemasons.[3]

The Reverend C. A. Grote received the honor of first assigned minister to the church, which was organized in 1856. Richard Grosse designed the church built on ten acres of donated land. Grosse owned a lumberyard and hardware store in Mason. A German immigrant himself, Grosse, trained builder, stonemason, and licensed architect, designed and built several prominent Mason County buildings, including a church in Hilda in addition to the church in Art.

The church sits firm and sure on the top of a rise overlooking Willow Creek. Framed by solid sandstone walls, rows of slim Gothic windows line each side. Two large, Gothic-arch double doors invite entry. The women entered through the north door on the right, men through the left. Once inside, seating following the entry custom, an unwritten tradition that gradually changed after World War II.

A massive bell, housed in the steeple-topped bell tower, provided a familiar sound to the German churchgoers. They heard church bells back in their homeland as their wake-up call in the morning and their call to rest in the evening. In German communities in Texas, the bells rang out for Sunday worship but also tolled as evening bells (*Abendglocken*) on Saturdays, a custom still followed in some rural Texas communities.

White lime-plaster walls lined the inside. The floor, pews, pulpit, and pump organ were all built of natural wood. Above the pulpit, an inscription painted in gold that read, "Gott ist die Liebe," meaning "God is love," has disappeared, possibly "because no one was able or willing to refurbish the old German lettering and symbols when the interior of the church was painted."[4]

FIRST UNITED METHODIST CHURCH

SAN MARCOS
Built in 1893

San Marcos and First United Methodist Church shared birthing process pains. Early settlers bought the Juan Martín Veramendi land grant for the town, and early settlers founded the church.

John D. Pitt, one of those first settlers, moved his family to the new settlement and began organizing the church. Pitt had help from Michael Sessom, who came to the area with an attachment of Texas Rangers. The church moved through the years, marking time in various facilities: Pitt's cabin, a shared community building, a wooden structure built in partnership with the local Masonic Order, a school, and finally its own brick building.

The brick building lasted nine years until its walls began to crumble, likely due to a fault under the church. The present day sanctuary constructed of cypress lumber was completed in 1893. It is described as "carpenter Gothic," a North American style of architecture referring to Gothic detailing elements applied to wooden structures built by locals or house carpenters.

Built in the shape of a cross, First Methodist takes pride in its design features that are still a part of the church: curved walnut pews, the pulpit and altar rail, and original beaded-board interior walls. "The present chandeliers hang from the original cast-iron medallions which feature cherubs in the central medallions. Cast-iron hymnal racks with hoops to hold walking canes are on the backs of the pews; and original wire hat holders for a gentlemen's hat can be found under certain pews," according to a *Wikipedia* entry on the church.

In an extensive renovation of the church in 1980–81, the four-story bell tower was reopened, providing a view of the bell.

Believed to be the oldest artifact in San Marcos, the bell was given to the church by a relative of Benjamin Hawkins, an Indian agent during George Washington's presidency. Originally it had hung in the chapel at Fort Hawkins in Macon, Georgia, a fort founded for the conversion of Native Americans.

CJChristensen '15

SAINTS PETER AND PAUL CATHOLIC CHURCH

NEW BRAUNFELS
Built in 1874

According to legend, a tribal chief's daughter had a vision beneath the spreading branches of an old oak tree on the north side of Saints Peter and Paul Catholic Church—a vision that helped free German settlers in Texas from the wrath of the Native Americans. "By this same oak, on Good Friday in 1845, Prince Solms of Braunfels, Germany, built a stockade to protect the settlers high on the bluff overlooking Comal Creek."[5] The hill was called *Lustiger Strumf* (happy stocking) because of its curved shape.

This first camp for the settlers, known as Zinkenburg, and named after Nicholas Zink, the surveyor who plotted the streets of New Braunfels, became the site of the first Catholic church. A temporary wood hut housed the church for two years. In 1849, Bishop Jean-Marie Odin, the Catholic prelate of Texas, arranged for the first permanent church building.

Constructed of black walnut, the church was called Saint Peter, Prince of the Apostles and was assigned a full-time priest. As the congregation grew, events of the Civil War and the challenges of frontier life prevented any building project. Finally in 1871, the cornerstone of what is the present church was laid.

Throughout the construction, services continued without interruption. The new structure surrounded and enclosed the "Walnut Church." Wagons brought local limestone to the site. Buttresses supported the walls at fifteen-foot intervals. When construction was completed in 1874, a notice in the local German newspapers announced that the wood would be auctioned off, and Walnut Church was removed through the new front door, one log at a time. Walnut Church became Saints Peter and Paul Catholic Church.

Keeping with structural authenticity, several remodels occurred over the decades. The storm-toppled church steeple was rebuilt in 1881, and a church clock added in 1889. In that same year, the open rafters in the interior were covered with metal, and the walls and ceilings painted gray and gold. A new Gothic altar was added, carved from walnut and ash. Wood replaced limestone floors in 1910, and new stained-glass windows were added.

The remodel in 1963 nearly doubled the size of the church, expanding the sanctuary, adding new pews, and simplifying the interior to give it a more contemporary feel of light and an uncluttered look. Keeping with the integrity of the exterior, stone taken from the old jail provided a uniform look.

Visitors today can spend time under the old oak, view the holy water fonts in the foyer made of stone from the original church, and see the fourteen stations of the cross, which are made of pressed paper that was imported from Holland in 1908. The sanctuary stands as it did in the 1874 church.

cjc
Carl Christensen '15

FIRST UNITED METHODIST CHURCH OF BARTLETT

BARTLETT
Built in 1921
Architect: Flanders and Flanders

Destroyed by a storm in 1894 and rebuilt that same year; destroyed by fire in 1896 and rebuilt again, First United Methodist Church of Bartlett could be knocked down, but not out. Originally known as the Indian Creek Church, the congregation moved to Bartlett between 1883 and 1885.

In its early days, congregants met in a store, school, and the local Baptist church; the first building was constructed in 1890 at a cost of $2,000. Then came the storm followed by the fire. The church building that was rebuilt in 1896 still stands today.

After the third rebuild, the congregation wanted to build a church large enough to sustain growth. A church revival kicked off a building campaign that lasted ten years and was plagued by financial difficulties.

Dallas architectural firm Flanders and Flanders accepted the church contract in May 1911, and construction began one year later. A one-time generous gift of $4,000 and a challenge of the congregation to raise an additional $2,000 cleared all debt. The church was dedicated June 19, 1921. Flanders's plan incorporated the existing structure with the new addition. Notable features include brick of mixed-earth tones, walls supported by double-stepped buttresses, and the Flanders's trademark towers at both the east and west corners of the north façade.

Churchgoers climb twelve steps, symbolic of the twelve disciples and twelve tribes of Israel, before entering double doors at each entrance. The raw bricks fired in community kilns were not uniformly heated, creating a pleasing palate of color variation. Darker bricks were incorporated into the wall to outline Gothic-arched windows and Gothic-arched dual entrances. Highly fired bricks, which were closer to brown, were used for the buttresses. Each of the towers is topped by an arched stained-glass window; the west entrance leading to the sanctuary also has the addition of the belfry with three arched windows

Inside the church, the roof truss pattern is unique in church architecture, with half of the truss system exposed below the sanctuary ceiling.

Throughout the years, the congregation committed to keeping the church maintained. A plethora of fundraising activities, ranging from bake sales to festivals to pancake suppers, have all contributed to this landmark church, one that did not give in to setbacks and still serves the congregation and community.

FIRST
ME CHURCH
SOUTH
cjchristensen '15

WESLEY AFRICAN METHODIST EPISCOPAL CHURCH

GEORGETOWN
Built in 1904

In the late 1860s, the African Methodist Episcopal Church assigned a group of fifteen men with little education to do missionary work in Texas. The men rode their ponies and preached across the state. One of those men, Richard Robert Haywood, was assigned to Austin and the surrounding area including Georgetown.

The Reverend Haywood organized Wesley Chapel African Methodist Episcopal Church in 1869. The church initially met in a tiny wood building. By the summer of 1904 the congregation, then under the leadership of the Reverend J. A. Jones, started work on fundraising for a new church. Everyone helped, including the children of the church. Mrs. Jones organized them into "the Nail Club," whose job was to raise money for all the nails needed for the new church.

Georgetown's mayor and other officials joined in dedicating the church, which was completed in time to host the African Methodist Episcopal Tenth District Conference in December 1904.

Wesley's simple frame construction is carpenter Gothic and includes a side tower and lancet window. Paneled oak double doors from England replaced the original doors in 1984. The original wood floors and ceiling remain, as well as solid-oak pews built by church member Jessie Chatman. Altar rails from the church have been preserved, but the original pulpit, also built by Chatman, now resides at Mood-Heritage Museum in Georgetown.

Preservation work continues. Wesley is one of the few historic buildings left in Georgetown's historically black neighborhood.

gjc
gchristensen '15

6

Historic Churches of South Texas

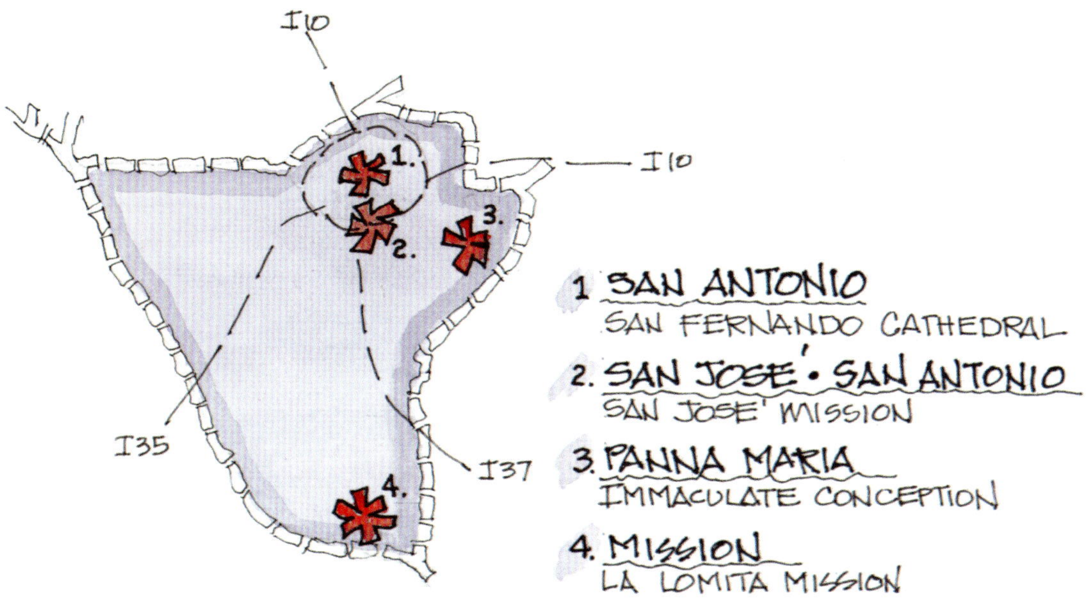

SAN FERNANDO CATHEDRAL

SAN ANTONIO
Built in 1755

Majestic in its façade, regal in its role as guardian of the city square, San Fernando Cathedral in San Antonio is the oldest active cathedral in the United States. It's also the oldest standing church building in Texas; the walls of the original church form the current sanctuary. Juan Antonio Pérez de Almazán, captain of the San Antonio presidio, selected the church site on July 2, 1731, laying out the central square of San Fernando de Béxar.

Fifty-six settlers transported from the Canary Islands had arrived in the area that year to establish a community and stop additional French expansion into Texas. Joining the military community, which had been in the area since 1718, the immigrants helped form the first organized civil government in Texas and build the church.

The cornerstone was likely laid on May 11, 1738, and the early church completed in 1755. The church dome was the landmark from which all mileage in Texas was measured.

San Fernando suffered flooding in 1819 and fire in 1828, requiring major improvements in 1829 and 1830. Records show that in 1831, James Bowie, a key player in the Texas Revolution, married Ursula María de Veramendi in the sanctuary. Mexican cannons perched on the church's roof during the Mexican siege of Bexar, and after the battle, Texans flew their victory flag. In 1836, General Antonio López de Santa Anna used the church as a lookout and hoisted the red flag of "no quarter" (no clemency for prisoners) from the church tower during the siege of the Alamo.

For almost ninety-five years, San Fernando served as the church for all of the religious denominations of San Antonio because Catholicism was the only recognized religion of the Spanish and Mexican governments prior to Texas' independence.

But after Texas gained her independence from Mexico, the Roman Catholic Church faced disarray, as evidenced by the colonial churches. Several missions had deteriorated. Half of San Fernando's roof was gone; swallows and bats were the main occupants.

An extensive renovation led by Franco-American architect Francois Giraud began in 1868. His design focused on a Gothic Revival nave, triple entry portals, a central rose window, and twin bell towers—a design quite similar to Notre Dame Cathedral in Paris. The new church was consecrated in 1873, with the second bell tower still under construction.

San Fernando was designated a cathedral with the formation of the Diocese of San Antonio in 1874. Renovations continued throughout the years. A renovation in 1936 unearthed a box of charred bones and other items, likely from the Battle of the Alamo. These items are now enshrined in the cathedral. Another major restoration occurred in the mid-1970s, and in 1987 repairs prepared the cathedral for a visit from Pope John Paul II, the only papal visit to Texas.

Presidents, governors, senators, and other dignitaries have visited San Fernando over the years. Majestic, regal, and a witness to Texas history, San Fernando, rich in heritage and beauty, continues to serve the people.

CJChristensen '14

MISSION SAN JOSÉ

SAN ANTONIO
Built in 1782

One of the five Spanish missions in San Antonio, Mission San José was "viewed as the model among the Texas missions and gained a reputation as a major social and cultural center. It became known as the 'Queen of the Missions.'"[1]

In 1720 Friar Antonio Margil de Jesús, a prominent Franciscan missionary, traveled to San Antonio and formally requested that a new mission be founded. With an abundance of wood available for beams and a local supply of limestone, the church design followed a square plan, similar to San Antonio de Valero Mission, known as the Alamo. Construction began in 1758 and completed in 1782.

Classified as Mexican Baroque, the church's original dome perched on a cylindrical support system, an unusual feature of Mexican colonial architecture. *Guardamelletas*—finger-like geometrical features—covered the façade. These figures were characteristic of the Mexican *Churrigueresque* style, named after a line of Spanish architect-sculptors in the 1600s from Barcelona. All were carved from golden tufa, a soft limestone that hardens with age.

One of the most striking features, *La Ventana de Rosa*, the Rose Window, represents a beautiful example of baroque architecture. Sculpted in 1775, the window opening is surrounded by delicate carvings of roses. The decorative framework is in the form of a quatrefoil, four partially overlapping circles. History supports Pedro Huízar as the artist in charge of the Rose Window and the façade, as well as the sculptor of the roses, which were possibly, according to legend, named for a lost love named Rosa or Rosita.

In 1794, the secularization of San José turned mission holdings over to the proprietors, including ninety-six mission Native Americans and also civilian settlers. The last Franciscan priest left in 1824, and Mission San José formally closed. Starting in 1813, troops had used the church and remaining out buildings intermittently, leaving behind heavy damage. Over the years various groups tried to use the church, but natural events and disuse took a toll. Storms in 1868 caused the collapse of part of the north wall, dome, and roof. The bell tower fell in 1903, but it was promptly rebuilt.

The Catholic Diocese, the San Antonio Conservation Society, Bexar County, the Work Projects Administration, the Civil Works Administration, and architect Harvey P. Smith began a major restoration starting in 1932. The church was rededicated in 1937, with ongoing restoration still in process. Mission San José is now part of the San Antonio Missions National Historical Park; the Archdiocese of San Antonio and San José Parish are charged with maintenance and preservation work on the church structure. Outlying buildings and grounds fall under park supervision.

Today, eighty percent of the church is restored to its original form. "Mission San José has become a symbol throughout the centuries for the Spanish mission frontier in Texas."[2]

CJC
Carl Christensen '15

IMMACULATE CONCEPTION CHURCH

PANNA MARIA
Built in 1877

"Come to Texas; life is good here." However the invitation was worded in his letters home, Father Leopold Moczygemba's open invitation to fellow Poles in the area of Silesia appealed to them. Conditions in 1850s Poland encouraged their thoughts of leaving: a poor economy, series of severe weather disasters, a lack of food, and cholera and typhoid outbreaks. It could only be better in Texas.

One hundred Silesian families, including four of Father Leopold's brothers, accepted the invitation. They traveled nine weeks by sea to Galveston. Disappointed that Leopold did not meet them, they hired carts for their belongings and walked the nearly two hundred miles to the junction of the San Antonio River and Cibolo Creek, forty-four miles southeast of San Antonio.

The group arrived on Christmas Eve, 1854, and Father Leopold immediately led them in a celebration mass at midnight under a large oak, which still guards the church today. Their Catholic faith proved to be the critical factor in maintaining their Polish identity. Just one year later, the church, named *Panna Maria,* meaning Virgin Mary in Polish, was completed.

Life in Poland had been difficult, but life in Texas held its own unique set of hardships. Unknowingly, Father Leopold had chosen an area that turned out to be a nesting place for rattlesnakes. Malaria, grasshoppers, floods, drought, and marauders also plagued the immigrants. The priest bore the brunt of their discouragement and blame.

Acknowledging their hardships, Father Leopold hosted a reconciliation banquet, promising the settlers the worst was behind them. During the dinner, a rattlesnake fell from the rafters onto the banquet table.

Then in 1856–57, the community endured fourteen months without rain. Father Leopold moved north and eventually settled in Michigan. Even as their church was destroyed by a lightning strike, the settlers refused to leave. A new church, which was built in 1877, solidified the commitment to their Texas home.

Built in the style of Silesian folk architecture, Panna Maria's steeple tower is marked by stringcourses—horizontal bands on a building, a traditional practice that helped lessen the weight on the foundation and added visual interest. Small gabled openings (lucarnes) surround the spire, and a botonée cross, with trefoils at each arm, tops the tower.

Today, Panna Maria is home to several valuable church artifacts, including a mosaic image of Our Lady of Czestochowa, Queen of Poland, called the *Black Madonna*. President Lyndon Johnson gave the image to Panna Maria to commemorate the millennium of Poland's Christianity.

During a recent renovation, it was discovered that the church has a painted ceiling. The ceiling has been restored to its original beauty. In 1974, Father Leopold's remains were reinterred under the live oak where he celebrated mass with that first group of Polish immigrants. The monument honoring him is dedicated to the "Patriarch of American Polonia." Panna Maria is the oldest Polish settlement in the United States, and the church carries the distinction of being the nation's first Polish church.

cjchristensen '15

LA LOMITA CHAPEL

MISSION
Built in 1899

The little chapel of La Lomita, torn down and rebuilt, damaged by neglect and a hurricane, and finally restored and preserved in a historic park, played a big role in the development of the Lower Rio Grande Valley.

Priests and ranch workers built the original adobe chapel in 1865; it lasted 20 years. By that time, the land around the chapel, which was part of two Spanish land grants, had been passed to two priests of the Missionary Oblates of Mary Immaculate. The Missionary Oblates, founded in France in 1816, arrived in Texas in 1894 to serve Catholics scattered across the Rio Grande Valley.

They built a headquarters in Brownsville and one in Roma, the farthest point inland reached by commercial riverboats. La Lomita Ranch served as the halfway stopping place where Oblates could spend the night. Their circuit rides on horseback lasted about six weeks each and took them more than one hundred miles into the heart of the Lower Rio Grande Valley.

The priests had hoped to establish a working ranch on the land, but eventually lack of success at ranching and raising crops moved the Oblates to designate the ranch as residential headquarters for a new Oblate mission district comprising all of Hildago County. The current chapel was built on the land in 1899.

With the arrival of the railroad, the Oblates realized the need for funds to establish churches and schools. They sold most of the La Lomita ranch property to developers who named the new town Mission, in honor of the Oblates and their service. With the move into town, the ranch and chapel facilities deteriorated from lack of use. In 1928, Father Chateau, the director of novitiate, repaired and refurnished the chapel as "a precious relic of the past."[3] A 1933 hurricane dealt the chapel a severe blow, but Father Chateau again repaired the building in 1939 so that it could once again be used for religious services.

The City of Mission arranged a lease agreement with the Oblates in 1965 and made La Lomita part of a municipal historical park. La Lomita stands today—small and humble, cared for and preserved—marking the important role it played in the history of the area and the commitment of the French Missionary Oblates to serve Catholics in the area.

cjchristensen '15

cjchristensen '15

7

Historic Churches of West Texas and the Panhandle

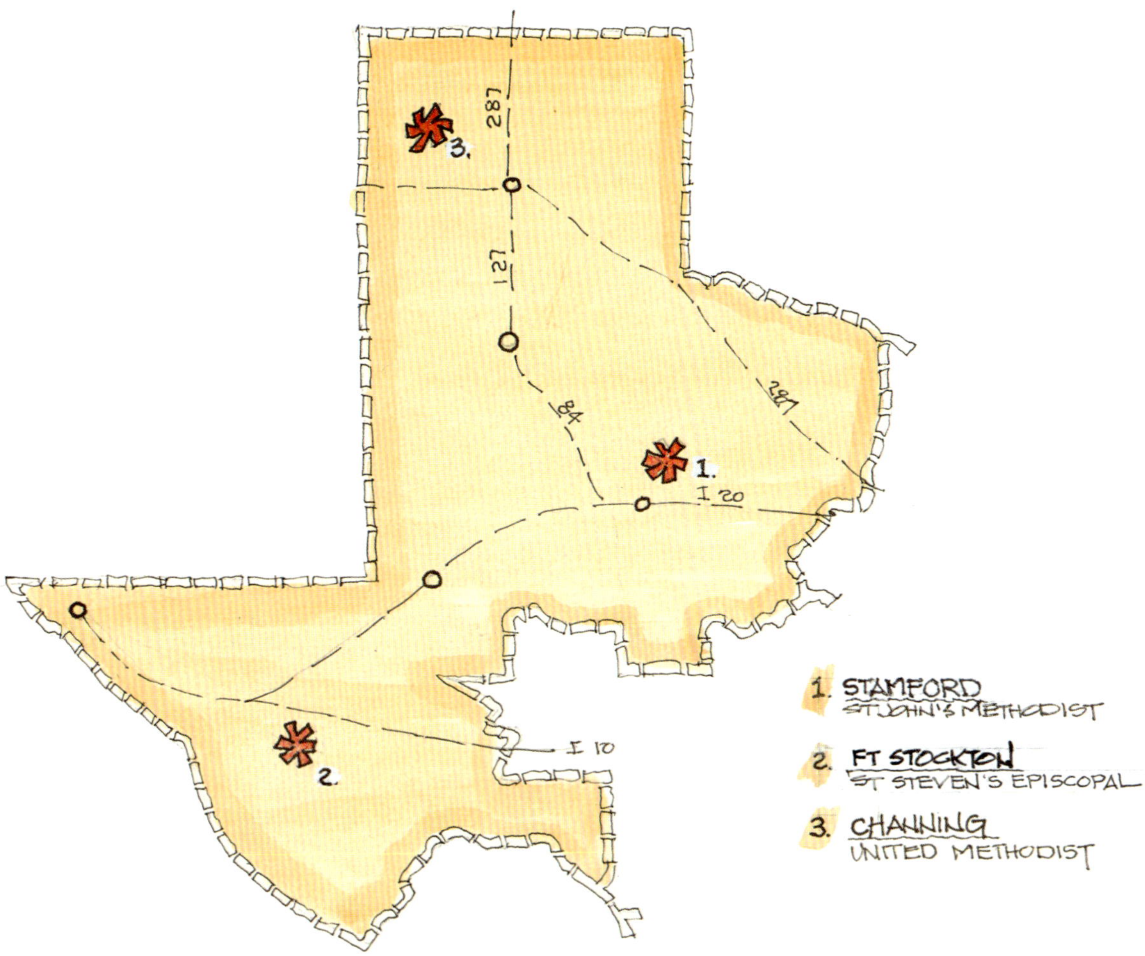

SAINT JOHN UNITED METHODIST CHURCH

STAMFORD
Built in 1910
Architect: James Flanders

For years Saint John United Methodist Church in Stamford boasted that its one hundred foot tower was the tallest between El Paso and Dallas. But Saint John's has more important credentials than its tower.

Built in 1910, Saint John's plan was nearly identical to Trinity Methodist Church of Dallas, which was often called architect James Edwards Flanders's masterpiece. Trinity was destroyed by fire in 1981. When construction was underway for Trinity in 1903, Stamford congregants had completed their meeting place, a small frame building. A mere seven years later, construction started on Stamford's new church with Flanders's design. The church took a direct tornado hit in 1912, adding two more years of work to complete the exterior. Funding became an issue.

Even though the church held services in the new building, it took another ten years of stop-and-go construction before the interior was complete. The church shows a variation of the central tower theme of Flanders with features inspired by the Prairie School style of architecture. An auditorium with seating for 1,290 was topped by an art glass dome. During extensive interior remodeling, the dome remained as the only original interior element.

Another distinguishing feature of the church is the Spanish *mixtilineo* window—a window shaped like a half quatrefoil.

Church archives document the original church specifications, which were written in 1909.

SAINT STEPHEN'S EPISCOPAL CHURCH

FORT STOCKTON
Built in 1896

Scheduled for demolition in 1956, it appeared that Saint Stephen's Episcopal Church would not be around for recognition with a historical marker. But the historic little church, known as the oldest existing Protestant church west of the Pecos River, was spared, thanks to a simple question.

Originally known as Saint Mark's, the church was built in Pecos in 1896 and hosted services until 1958. That year, the Pecos congregation started construction on a new church building, and the fate of the historic church was unclear. In Fort Stockton, the Episcopal Church community had been meeting in Dr. D. J. Sibley's office because they had no building of their own and shared a priest with the Pecos church. It was the priest who alerted the Fort Stockton congregants that the Pecos church was going to be torn down.

Dr. Sibley and his wife Jane agreed the idea didn't sound good to them and asked the priest if he'd consider donating the Pecos church to the Fort Stockton Episcopalians. The Pecos church agreed to the donation if the Fort Stockton church would cover costs. The Sibleys donated an acre of land for the church's new home.

The move required two flatbed trucks and a crane to remove the steeple and place it on a different truck from the structure. Built in the style of English country churches, Saint Stephen's exterior was charming. The interior was not in good shape, so three members of the congregation with art backgrounds, including Mrs. Sibley, went to work. The inside was white washed and new pews ordered. Antique paper, a faux stained-glass pattern, was ordered from Brussels to cover the windows. A silver designer handcrafted the chalice and designed a black ebony cross.

According to Mrs. Sibley, "We went for an artistic impression and it all turned out just beautifully—simple and exquisite. . . . We all felt we had reclaimed a jewel."[1]

Today, Saint Stephen's remains an active church and is stop number fifteen on the Fort Stockton Chamber of Commerce's tour of historical sites. The additional historical marker, underneath the main marker, corrects two errors on the original historical marker: the land was donated by both Dr. and Mrs. Sibley, and the church was given, not sold, by the Pecos congregation.

UNITED METHODIST CHURCH

CHANNING
Built in 1902

In the Panhandle of Texas, where the dust is plentiful and the rain scarce, Channing owes its roots to the founding of the XIT Ranch, once one of the largest cattle ranches in Texas. Channing served as general headquarters and supplier for the XIT. John V. Farwell, who along with his brother Charles B. Farwell, started the ranch, founded the United Methodist Church, along with Rev. E. T. Harrison, to minister to ranch personnel.

Early church members included A. G. Boyce, manager of the XIT, his wife Annie, and their daughter Bessie. The church was completed in 1902 and holds the honor of being the first Methodist church north of the Canadian River.

Although unsubstantiated, the story goes that the church bell was donated to the Channing church by a church in nearby Clarendon. The cowboys belonging to the Channing church rode on horseback to get the bell, but they discovered the people in Clarendon had changed their minds. Not to be deterred in their mission, guns were drawn, and the bell was brought successfully to the Channing church.

Today, the church bell still rings. Most of the ranch hands and cowboys have moved on to the local Cowboy Church, but the little church serves the people of Channing and Dalhart. According to one member, "If you have fifteen people on Sunday, it's a crowd."

echristensen '14

NOTES

Preface

1. Fehrenbach, *Lone Star: A History of Texas and the Texans*, 599.

2. Willard B. Robinson, "Church Architecture," *Handbook of Texas Online*, (http://www.tshaonline.org/handbook/online/articles/cgc02). Uploaded on June 12, 2010. Published by the Texas State Historical Association.

3. Lich, *The German Texans*, 6.

4. Ibid., 9.

5. Clinton Machann, "Czechs," Handbook of Texas Online (http://www.tshaonline.org/handbook/online/articles/plc02). Last modified on July 29, 2014. Published by the Texas State Historical Association.

6. McQueen, *Black Churches in Texas: A Guide to Historic Congregations*, 3.

Historic Churches of the Texas Gulf Coast

1. "History of the Mother Church of Texas," Reedy Chapel, http://reedychapel.com/about-us/history.

2. "A Brief History," Grace Episcopal Church, http://www.gracechurchgalveston.org/history.htm.

3. Grace Episcopal Church. *Tour pamphlet*, 6.

4. "About Us," Wallis, Texas, http://www.wallistexas.org/about.htm.

Historic Churches of East Texas

1. Robinson, *Reflections of Faith Houses of Worship in the Lone Star State*, 83.

2. "Narrative for The Union Missionary Baptist Church, Jefferson, Texas," Marion County Historical Commission, http://www.caddolake-nha.com/RTHL%20Narrative.pdf, 5.

3. Robinson, *Reflections of Faith, Houses of Worship in the Lone Star State*, 116.

4. Selden, *Seven Score and Ten, One Hundred Fifty Years of The Presbyterian Church in Palestine, Texas*, 84–85.

5. Tiffany Patterson, *Rural Churches of Callaway County*, (Jefferson: Missouri State Historic Preservation Office, July 2010). 19.

6. Clara Malak, "Saint Joseph Catholic Church History," Saint Joseph Catholic Church, December 1999, http://www.stjosephnewwaverlytx.net/About%20Us/St.%20Joseph%20History2.html.

Historic Churches of North Central Texas

1. Robinson *Reflections of Faith, Houses of Worship in the Lone Star State*, 104.

2. Elroy Christenson, "The Scandinavians of Bosque Co. Texas," www.ElroyChristenson.com, last modified November 10, 2014, www.next1000.com/family/EC/scand.TX.html.

3. "Saint Mary's Protestant Episcopal Church," *The Hamilton County News*, June 29, 1934, http://freepages.genealogy.rootsweb.ancestry.com/~gazetteer2000/news1934/st_mary.htm.

4. Reverend Brad Dardaganian, "Living our Legacy," First Presbyterian Church, http://www.fpc-bonham.org/living-our-legacy.

5. "History—The Foundation of a Parish," Saint Peter Catholic Church, Lindsay, Texas, http://stpeterlindsay.org/history.

6. Rabbi James L. Kessler, "Jews," *Handbook of Texas Online* (http://www.tshaonline.org/handbook/online/articles/pxj01), accessed August 12, 2015. Uploaded on June 15, 2010. Published by the Texas State Historical Association.

7. Ibid.

8. Jeanie Allen Davis, "Little Green Church remains active," *The Kaufman Herald*, February 9, 2006.

Historic Churches of South Central Texas

1. "Historical Churches," Lockhart Chamber of Commerce, http://www.lockhartchamber.com/pages/HistoricalChurches.

2. "Sanctuary History," Emmanuel Episcopal Church, http://www.episcopal-lockhart.org/history.html.

Historic Churches of the Hill Country

1. Kenn Knopp, "A Short History of New Saint Mary's Church," KLRU: The Painted Churches of Texas: Echoes of the Homeland, http://www.klru.org/paintedchurches/fredericksburg.html, 2009.

2. "The First Hundred Years, A History of Grace Episcopal Church," Brochure by Grace Episcopal Church, Llano, Texas.

3. Art Methodist Church, http://voicesofthetexashills.org/vthchurch0022.htm, accessed January 2014.

4. Jordan, *Yesterday in the Texas Hill Country*, 73.

5. "Saints Peter & Paul Catholic Church, A Self-Guided Tour," Brochure by Saints Peter & Paul Catholic Church, New Braunfels, Texas.

Historic Churches of South Texas

1. "Mission San José y San Miguel de Aguayo" National Park Service, http://www.nps.gov/saan/learn/historyculture/sanjosehistory1.htm, accessed May 2015.

2. Ibid.

3. Robert E. Wright, O.M.I., "La Lomita Mission," *Handbook of Texas Online* (http://www.tshaonline.org/handbook/online/articles/uql07). Uploaded on June 15, 2010. Published by the Texas State Historical Association.

Historic Churches of West Texas and the Panhandle

1. Sibley, *Jane's Window, My Spirited Life in West Texas and Austin*, 106.

GLOSSARY

Prairie School. The Prairie School style architecture is usually marked by its integration with the surrounding landscape, as well as horizontal lines, flat or hipped roofs with broad eaves, windows assembled in horizontal bands, solid construction, craftsmanship, and restraint in the use of decoration. (www.prairieschoolarchitecture.com)

Mixtilíneo. A type of arch based upon a half quatrefoil.

Gothic style. A medieval mode of the thirteenth, fourteenth, and fifteenth centuries in Europe, characterized by pointed arches, buttresses, and tracery.

Victorian. A period of art coinciding with the reign of Queen Victoria (1837–1901); in America, loosely the last part of the nineteenth century.

Trefoil. An architectural ornament in the shape of three arcs arranged in a circle. (www.memidex.com/trefoil+architectural-ornament)

Renaissance Revival. A style with a decorative vocabulary based on the architecture of the Renaissance.

Gothic Revival. A style in which architectural features were patterned after Gothic work.

Lancet. A pointed arch with radii of segments of curvature equal to or greater than the width of the opening.

Cruciform. Shaped in the form of a cross.

Italianate. Often included in the so-called Picturesque Movement, the Italianate style began in England as a reaction to the rigid formalism that had come to dominate nineteenth-century architecture. (www.wentworthstudio.com/historic-styles/italianate/)

Reredos. A wall forming a backdrop for an altar.

Entablature. In Classical architecture, the group of components surmounting a wall, set of columns, or pilasters.

Carpenter Gothic. A style with forms and details constructed from wood, derived from medieval architecture.

Vernacular architecture. Composed of local materials and derived from local customs, using techniques that have been passed on from generation to generation. (www.archdaily.com/tag/vernacular-architecture/)

Basilican plan. Developed in ancient Rome, this layout consists of a rectangular plan, incorporating a nave and side aisles. It was adopted by early Christians for churches.

Romanesque Revival. A nineteenth and early-twentieth-century style of architecture in which European work of the eleventh through the thirteenth centuries provided the models; a hallmark of the style if the Roman arch.

Akron plan. For church buildings, this plan was popularized by architectural pattern books in the United States in the late nineteenth and early twentieth centuries. The plan is typified by an auditorium form worship space (the "rotunda"), surrounded by connecting Sunday school classrooms spaces on one or two levels. The plan promotes efficiency of movement by congregants between worship and Sunday School. The plan was first used in 1872 at the First Methodist Episcopal Church in Akron, Ohio, in a design by philanthropist Lewis Miller, Walter Blythe, and architect Jacob Snyder. (https://en.wikipedia.org/wiki/Akron_Plan)

Byzantine style. A type of architecture derived from ancient Roman architecture, before Christ, characterized by arches, domes, and polychromatic decorative work. It is still employed in Greek churches.

Queen Anne. Of the various Victorian styles of architecture, one of the most important that continued from the nineteenth century into the first two decades of the twentieth century was the Queen Anne. Popular from about 1860 to 1890 in England and somewhat later in the United States, the Queen Anne style lent itself to the excesses of the Victorian age with its turrets, oriel windows, and medieval influences. Beloved by lumber barons, many of the largest and most spectacular homes of the early twentieth century were built in this style. (http://www.antiquehome.org/Architectural-Style/queen-anne.htm)

Stringcourses. A continuous molding on an exterior wall.

Lucarne. A small opening in a spire, capped with a gablet (miniature gable).

Guardamelletas. In Spanish architecture, a decorative feature with fingers pointing downward.

Baroque. A style characterized by elaborate decoration developed during the late Renaissance.

Unless otherwise noted, all definitions are taken from Willard B. Robinson's 1994 book, *Reflections of Faith, Houses of Worship in the Lone Star State.*

BIBLIOGRAPHY

Books

Calvert, Robert A., Arnoldo De Leon, and Gregg Cantrell, *The History of Texas*. Wheeling, Il.: Harlan Davidson, Inc., 2007, Fourth Edition.

Fehrenbach, T.R., *Lone Star, A History of Texas and the Texans*. New York: Collier Books, 1980.

Henry, Jay C., *Architecture in Texas, 1895–1945*. Austin: University of Texas Press, 1993.

Jordan, Gilbert J., *Yesterday in the Texas Hill Country*. College Station: Texas A&M University Press, 1995.

Lich, Glen E., *The German Texans*. San Antonio: The University of Texas, Institute of Texan Cultures, 1996. Revised Edition.

McQueen, Clyde, *Black Churches in Texas, A Guide to Historic Congregations*. College Station: Texas A&M University Press, 2000.

Myers, Lois E., and Rebecca Sharpless, *Rock Beneath the Sand, Country Churches in Texas*. College Station: Texas A&M University Press, 2003.

Selden, Jack, *Seven Score and Ten, One Hundred Fifty Years of the Presbyterian Church in Palestine, Texas*. Palestine: Clacton Press, 1999.

Sibley, Jane Dunn, as told to Jim Comer, *Jane's Window, My Spirited Life in West Texas and Austin*. College Station: Texas A&M University Press, 2013.

Robinson, Willard B., *Reflections of Faith, Houses of Worship in the Lone Star State*. Waco: Baylor University Press, 1994.

Other Printed Resources

"Celebrating 100 Years of the Cornerstone—Guardian Angel Catholic Church." Church of the Guardian Angel booklet.

"Church of the Visitation." Westphalia Historical Society, Inc. booklet.

Davis, Jeanie Allen. "'Little Green Church' Remains Active," *Kaufman Herald*, February 9, 2006.

"Grace Episcopal Church Galveston, Texas." Grace Episcopal Church booklet.

"Grace Episcopal Church: The First Hundred Years." Grace Episcopal Church booklet.

"The Historical New Sweden Evangelical Lutheran Church." New Sweden Evangelical Lutheran Church booklet.

"Lutcher Memorial Building First Presbyterian Church." First Presbyterian Church booklet.

Milton, Maly A. "This Church at Wesley," *New Ulm Enterprise*, September, 1996.

"A Memorial Tribute to our Silesian Polish Immigrant Ancestors," Panna Maria Heritage Center booklet.

"Our Merciful Saviour Episcopal Church Kaufman." Our Merciful Saviour Episcopal Church booklet.

"Panna Maria, Texas, the Oldest Polish Settlement in the USA." Immaculate Conception Church booklet.

"Sts Peter & Paul Catholic Church A Self-Guided Tour." Saints Peter and Paul Catholic Church booklet.

"Welcome to St Mary's Catholic Church, Walking Tour of Our Parish Church." Lay Missionaries of Charity booklet.

"Welcome St. Mary's Catholic Church Fredericksburg." Saint Mary's Catholic Church booklet.

Interviews

Duke Delaware (Local historian, Cumberland Presbyterian, Jefferson), in interview with the author, February 2013.

Ken Fridrich (Pastor, Hilda Methodist Church, Mason), in interview with the author, January 19, 2014.

Randy Frye (Pastor, First Christian Church, Lockhart) in interview with the author, March 2015.

Elaine Howard (Historian, Our Merciful Saviour Episcopal Church, Kaufman), in interview with the author, April 2014.

Michael Koehn (Local historian, Wesley Brethren Church), in interview with the author, November 2014.

Nora Teague (Historian, Saint Mary's Episcopal Church, Hamilton) in interview with the author, February 2015.

Doris Voltin (Church of the Visitation), interview with the author, February 2015.

Web Resources

GULF

Saint Joseph's

Galveston Historical Foundation. "1859 St. Joseph's Church." http://www.galvestonhistory.org/attractions/architectural-heritage/st-josephs-church.

Galveston.com & Company, Inc. "1859 St. Joseph Church." www.galveston.com/stjosephchurch.

Reedy Chapel

Bryant-Honors, Salatheia. "Galveston's historic Reedy Chapel A.M.E. is battered and bruised, but it will survive Ike." *Houston Chronicle*, September 19, 2008. www.chron.com/life/houston-belief/article/Galveston-s-historic-Reedy-Chapel-A-M-E-is-1784745.php.

Hardman, Peggy. "Reedy Chapel African Methodist Episcopal Church," *Handbook of Texas Online*. http://www.tshaonline.org/handbook/online/articles/imr01, accessed September 01, 2015. Uploaded on June 15, 2010. Published by the Texas State Historical Association.

Reedy Chapel. "Standing Strong at 165 years old." http://reedychapel.com.

Guardian Angel Catholic Church Wallis

Sherman, George. "Guardian Angel Church turns 100." *Texas Catholic Herald News*, April 30, 2013. www.archgh.org/default.asp?id=500&hid=1370.

"The Guardian Angel Church." *Texas Escapes Online Magazine*. July 7, 2008. www.texasescapes.com/Churches/Wallis-Texas-Churches.htm.

Grace Episcopal

]Grace Episcopal Church. "A Brief History." January 15, 2010. www.gracechurchgalveston.org/history.htm.

First Presbyterian Church

First Presbyterian Church. www.firstpresorange.com.

Pipe Organs. "Casavant Freres." http://pipeorgans.wikia.com/wiki/Casavant_Fr%C3%A8res.

Nienke, William, and Sam Morrow. "Lutcher Memorial Church Building." www.9key.com/markers/marker_detail.asp?atlas_number=5361011496.

Annunciation Catholic Church

O'Donnell, Sister Mary Brendan. "Church of the Annunciation, Houston," *Handbook of Texas Online*. http://www.tshaonline.org/handbook/online/articles/ivc01, accessed September 1, 2015. Uploaded on June 12, 2010. Published by the Texas State Historical Association.

Christ Episcopal Church

Christ Episcopal Church. "Christ Episcopal Church." Uploaded November 3, 2010. http://freepages.history.rootsweb.ancestry.com/~christepiscopal/history.htm.

Matagorda Area Chamber of Commerce. "History." www.matagordachamber.com/history.php.

Antioch Missionary Baptist Church

BlackPast.org "Antioch Missionary Baptist Church, Houston, Texas." http://www.blackpast.org/aaw/antioch-missionary-baptist-church-houston-texas-1868.

Antioch Missionary Baptist Church. "A Brief History." http://www.ambchouston.org/index.php/about-us/brief-history.

Nienke, William, and Sam Morrow. "Antioch Missionary Baptist Church, Houston, Harris County, Texas." Accessed May 2015. www.9key.com/markers/marker_detail.asp?atlas_number=5201010597.

WEST TEXAS AND THE PANHANDLE

Saint Stephen's Episcopal

Saint Stephen's Episcopal Church. "St. Stephen's Welcomes You." Accessed April 2015. http://fsepiscopalchurch.org.

Channing United Methodist Church Channing

"Texas Churches, Channing United Methodist Church." *Texas Escapes Online Magazine*, July 14, 2010. http://www.texasescapes.com/Churches/Channing-United-Methodist-Church-Channing-Texas.htm.

St. John's Methodist Church Stamford

"Stamford, Texas." *Texas Escapes Online Magazine*. Accessed April 2015. http://www.texasescapes.com/TexasPanhandleTowns/Stamford-Texas.htm.

SOUTH

Mission San José

Cruz, Gilberto R. "San José y San Miguel de Aguayo Mission," *Handbook of Texas Online*. http://www.tshaonline.org/handbook/online/articles/uqs23, accessed September 07, 2015. Last modified on September 7, 2011. Published by the Texas State Historical Association.

Las Misiones. "Mission San José." Accessed April 2015. http://oldspanishmissions.org/mission-san-jose.

National Park Service. "Mission San José y San Miguel de Aguayo." Accessed September 5, 2015. http://www.nps.gov/saan/learn/historyculture/sanjosehistory1.htm.

La Lomita Chapel Mission

MissionTexas.net. "History of the area around La Lomita near

Mission, TX." Accessed April 2015. http://www.missiontexas.net/history/la-lomita.

"La Lomita, Texas." *Texas Escapes Online Magazine*, January 30, 2009. http://www.texasescapes.com/SouthTexasTowns/La-Lomita.htm.

"La Lomita Chapel." *Texas Escapes Online Magazine*, September 7, 2007. http://www.texasescapes.com/Churches/La-Lomita-Chapel-Texas.htm

Wright, Robert E. O.M.I. "La Lomita Mission," *Handbook of Texas Online*. http://www.tshaonline.org/handbook/online/articles/uq107, accessed September 07, 2015. Uploaded on June 15, 2010. Published by the Texas State Historical Association.

San Fernando Cathedral

Wikipedia. "Cathedral of San Fernando." Accessed August 20, 2015. http://en.wikipedia.org/wiki/Cathedral_of_San_Fernando.

Gaines, Ann Graham. "San Fernando Cathedral," *Handbook of Texas Online*. http://www.tshaonline.org/handbook/online/articles/ivs01, accessed September 7, 2015. Uploaded on June 15, 2010. Published by the Texas State Historical Association.

ExploreSouthernHistory.com. "San Fernando Cathedral, San Antonio, Texas." Accessed April 2015. http://www.exploresouthernhistory.com/sanfernando.html.

Immaculate Conception Catholic Church

Panna Maria Historical Society. "About Panna Maria." http://pannamariatexas.com/OurPolishSettlement.htm.

Temple, Louann Atkins. "Panna Maria, TX," *Handbook of Texas Online*. http://www.tshaonline.org/handbook/online/articles/hlp04, accessed September 7, 2015. Uploaded on June 15, 2010. Published by the Texas State Historical Association.

Coppedge, Clay. "A Snakebitten Legacy, Father Leopold Moczygemba." *Texas Escapes Online Magazine*. September 17, 2012. http://www.texasescapes.com/ClayCoppedge/Snakebitten-Legacy.htm.

"Panna Maria, Texas." *Texas Escapes Online Magazine*, accessed April 2015. http://www.texasescapes.com/TexasGhostTowns/PannaMariaTexas/PannaMariaTx.htm.

SOUTH CENTRAL

Saint Mary's Catholic Church

"St. Mary's Catholic Church." *Texas Escapes Online Magazine*, accessed April 2015. http://www.texasescapes.com/Churches/Plantersville-Texas-Painted-Church-St-Marys.htm.

Saint Mary/Saint Joseph Catholic Community. "History of St. Mary's Catholic Church." Accessed April 2015. http://smsj.org/st-marys-plantersville.

Saint James Episcopal

Saint James Episcopal and Preschool. "The Church and its Furnishings." Accessed March 2015. http://stjameslagrange.org/history.

Saints Cyril and Methodius Church

Oakes, Alan. "Dubina: Giant Oaks from Acorns Grow." KLRU: The Painted Churches of Texas: Echoes of the Homeland, http://www.klru.org/paintedchurches/dubina.html.

Wikipedia. "Dubina, Texas." http://en.wikipedia.org/wiki/Dubina,_Texas.

"Saints Cyril and Methodius Church." *Texas Escapes Online Magazine*, accessed March 2015. http://www.texasescapes.com/CentralTexasTownsSouth/DubinaTexas/Dubina-Texas-Painted-Saints-Cyril-and-Methodius-Church.htm.

Independence Baptist Church

Hesler, Samuel B. "Independence Baptist Church," *Handbook of Texas Online*, http://www.tshaonline.org/handbook/online/articles/ivi01, accessed September 7, 2015. Uploaded on June 15, 2010. Published by the Texas State Historical Association.

Independence Preservation Trust. "Independence Baptist Church." Accessed February 2015. http://www.independencetx.com/IndependenceBaptistChurch.htm.

Liberty Baptist Church

StoppingPoints.com. "Liberty Baptist Church." Accessed February 2015. http://www.stoppingpoints.com/texas/sights.cgi?marker=Liberty+Baptist+Church&cnty=washington.

Independence Preservation Trust. "Liberty Baptist Church." Accessed February 2015. http://www.independencetx.com/LibertyBaptistChurch.htm.

Wesley Brethren Church

Unity of the Brethren Church. "Wesley." Accessed March 2015. http://unityofthebrethren.org/congregations/wesley.

Oakes, Alan. "Wesley Brethren: The Former Schoolhouse." KLRU: The Painted Churches of Texas: Echoes of the Homeland. http://www.klru.org/paintedchurches/wesley.html

StoppingPoints.com. "Wesley Brethren Church." http://www

.stoppingpoints.com/texas/sights.cgi?marker=Wesley+Brethren+Church&cnty=washington.

First Christian Church

StoppingPoints.com "First Christian Church (Disciples of Christ) of Lockhart."

http://www.stoppingpoints.com/texas/sights.cgi?marker=First+Christian+Church+(Disciples+of+Christ)+of+Lockhart&cnty=caldwell.

Waymarking.com "First Christian Church (Disciples of Christ) of Lockhart. http://www.waymarking.com/waymarks/WM104F_First_Christian_Church_Disciples_of_Christ.

Lockhart Chamber of Commerce. "Historical Churches." Accessed February 2015. http://www.lockhartchamber.com/pages/HistoricalChurches.

Emmanuel Episcopal Church

Emmanuel Episcopal Church. "History." Accessed February 2015. http://www.episcopal-lockhart.org/history.html.

Church of the Visitation

Church of the Visitation. "History of Our Parish." Accessed February 2015. http://churchofthevisitation.org/history.shtm.

Saint Paul Lutheran Church

Texas Wendish Heritage Society. "Museum." Accessed April 2015. http://www.texaswendish.org/Pages/Museum.aspx.

Oakes, Alan. "Servin: The Culture of the Wends." KLRU: The Painted Churches of Texas: Echoes of the Homeland. Accessed April 2015. http://www.klru.org/paintedchurches/serbin.html.

Grider, Sylvia. "Wends," *Handbook of Texas Online*. http://www.tshaonline.org/handbook/online/articles/plw01, accessed September 7, 2015. Uploaded on June 15, 2010. Published by the Texas State Historical Association.

St. Mary's Church of the Assumption

Oakes, Alan. "Praha." KLRU: The Painted Churches of Texas: Echoes of the Homeland. Accessed February 2015. http://www.klru.org/paintedchurches/praha.html.

The Greater Schulenburg Chamber of Commerce. "Painted Churches." Accessed February 2015. http://schulenburgchamber.org/tours/churches.

Lotto, F., "Fayette County, Her History and Her People: Praha," 1902. The Fayette County TXGenWeb Project. http://www.fayettecountyhistory.org/praha.htm.

Janecka, Ed. "Praha, TX," *Handbook of Texas Online*. http://www.tshaonline.org/handbook/online/articles/hnp51, accessed September 7, 2015. Uploaded on June 15, 2010. Published by the Texas State Historical Association.

NORTH CENTRAL

First Presbyterian Church

First Presbyterian Church—Bonham, Texas. "Living our Legacy—Notes for the Dedication of First Presbyterian Church, Bonham." Accessed March 2015. http://www.fpc-bonham.org/category/living-our-legacy.

Fannin County Historical Commission. "Historical Markers in Fannin County." Accessed March 2015. http://www.fannincountyhistory.org/first-presbyterian-church-bonham.html.

Our Merciful Savior Episcopal

Our Merciful Saviour Episcopal Church. Accessed March 2015. http://www.omschurch.org/about.

Saint Paul United Church of Christ

StoppingPoints.com. "St. Paul United Church of Christ." Accessed July 15, 2015. http://www.stoppingpoints.com/texas/sights.cgi?marker=St.+Paul+United+Church+of+Christ&cnty=falls.

First United Methodist Church of Marlin

Nienke, William, and Sam Morrow. "First United Church of Marlin—Marlin, Falls County, Texas." Accessed March 2015. http://www.9key.com/markers/marker_detail.asp?atlas_number=5145008833.

Marlin Chamber of Commerce and Historic Downtown Marlin Association. "The History of Marlin, Texas." Accessed March 2015. http://marlintexas.com/temp/history.htm.

First United Methodist Church of Royse City

First United Methodist Church of Royse City. "Our History." Accessed March 2015. http://www.fumcroysecity.org/about/our-history.

McKenzie United Methodist Church

McKenzie United Methodist Church. "McKenzie UMC History." Accessed March 2015. http://www.mckenzieumc.com/about-us/church-history.html.

"Honey Grove Churches." *Texas Escapes Online Magazine*, May 6, 2008. http://www.texasescapes.com/Churches/Honey-Grove-Texas-Churches.htm.

Honey Grove Preservation League. "Saving and Documenting the History of Honey Grove, Texas." Accessed February 2015. http://www.honeygrovepreservation.org/mckenzie-methodist-church.html.

Our Savior Lutheran

City of Clifton. "Norse Historic District." Accessed March 2015. http://www.visitclifton.org/page/norse-historic-district.aspx.

Duncan, Patricia L. "Norse, TX," *Handbook of Texas Online* http://www.tshaonline.org/handbook/online/articles/hln26, accessed September 7, 2015. Uploaded on June 15, 2010. Published by the Texas State Historical Association.

Our Savior's Lutheran Church at Norse. "The History of Our Savior's Lutheran Church at Norse." Accessed March 2015. http://oursaviorsnorse.org.

SAINT OLAF (THE ROCK CHURCH)

Christenson, Elroy. "The Scandinavians of Bosque Co. Texas," www.ElroyChristenson.com. Last modified November 10, 2014. www.next1000.com/family/EC/scand.TX.html.

Saint Olaf Lutheran Church. "St. Olaf, A Brief History." Accessed March 2015. http://www.saintolaflutheran.org/history.html.

SAINT PETER CATHOLIC CHURCH

Saint Peter Catholic Church. "History: The Foundation of a Parish." Accessed April 2015. http://stpeterlindsay.org/history.

McDaniel, Robert Wayne. "Lindsay, TX," *Handbook of Texas Online* http://www.tshaonline.org/handbook/online/articles/h1144, accessed September 7, 2015. Uploaded on June 15, 2010. Published by the Texas State Historical Association.

Haskins, Jason John Paul. "Pained Churches of Texas: St. Peter, Lindsay." *Locus Iste*. November 15, 2013. http://locusiste.org/blog/2013/11/painted-churches-of-texas-st-peter-lindsay.

SAINT MARY'S EPISCOPAL

Booth, Thomas. "History of St. Mary's Protestant Episcopal Church." *The Hamilton County News*, June 29, 1934. http://freepages.genealogy.rootsweb.ancestry.com/~gazetteer2000/news1934/st_mary.htm.

Emmanuel Lutheran Church

Emanuel Lutheran Church. "History." Accessed April 2015. http://www.emanueldallas.org/pages/history.html.

TEMPLE BETH EL

East Texas Historical Association. "1992 Terry Winner—Temple Beth El, Corsicana, TX." Accessed April 2015. http://www.easttexashistorical.org/v3/programs/terry/terry_1992_temple.html.

Wikipedia. "Temple Beth-El (Corsicana, TX)." Last modified May 26, 2014. http://en.wikipedia.org/wiki/Temple_Beth-El_%28Corsicana%2c_Texas%29

Kessler, Rabbi James L. "Jews," *Handbook of Texas Online* http://www.tshaonline.org/handbook/online/articles/pxj01, accessed September 7, 2015. Uploaded on June 15, 2010. Published by the Texas State Historical Association.

Goldring/Woldenberg Institute of Southern Jewish Life. "Encyclopedia of Southern Jewish Communities—Corsicana, TX." Accessed May 2015. http://www.isjl.org/texas-corsicana-encyclopedia.html.

HILL COUNTRY

NEW SWEDEN LUTHERAN CHURCH

New Sweden Evangelical Lutheran Church. "About Us—Our History." Accessed February 2015. http://newswedenelca.org/taxonomy/term/7.

Stucco, Johnson. "The Most Photographed Church in Texas." *Texas Escapes Online Magazine*, January 22, 2010. http://texasescapes.com/Churches/The-Most-Photographed-Church-in-Texas.htm.

Meyer, Bill. "New Sweden Evangelical Lutheran Church." *The Blackland Reporter*, May 19, 2012. http://blacklandreporter.com/new-sweden-evangelical-lutheran-church.

WESLEY CHAPEL AME CHURCH

Williamson Historical Commission. "Wesley Chapel A.M.E. Church Historical Marker." Accessed February 2015. http://www.williamson-county-historical-commission.org/GEORGETOWN_TEXAS/Wesley_Chapel_A-M-E_Church_Historical_Marker_Williamson_county_Texas.html.

SAINT STANISLAUS CATHOLIC CHURCH

Saint Stanislaus Catholic Church. "A History of Our Church." http://www.ststanislausbandera.com/history.html.

Browne, Byron. "Bandera, Texas." *Texas Escapes Online Magazine*, March 11, 2010. http://www.texasescapes.com/TRIPS/Bandera-Texas.htm.

Goodley, Elenora Dugosh, "Emigration of Bandera Texas Polish Settlers." Polish Texans, July 15, 2010. http://www.polish-texans.com/2010/07/emigration-of-bandera-texas-polish-silesians.

POLLY'S CHAPEL

Polly Texas Pioneer Association. "Polly's Chapel." Accessed March 2015. http://www.pollytexaspioneerassociation.org/Polly_s_Chapel.html.

Browne, Byron. "Bandera, Texas." *Texas Escapes Online Magazine*, March 11, 2010. http://www.texasescapes.com/TRIPS/Bandera-Texas.htm.

FIRST UNITED METHODIST CHURCH SAN MARCOS

Wikipedia. "First United Methodist Church (San Marcos, Texas)." Last modified January 27, 2015. http://

en.wikipedia.org/wiki/First_United_Methodist_Church_(San_Marcos,_Texas)

Hernandez, Alison. "First UMC San Marcos, History." Partners for Sacred Places. Last modified September 18, 2013. https://sites.google.com/a/sacredplaces.org/texas-sacred-places-project/system/app/pages/search?scope=search-site&q=First+UMC+San+Marcos.

HILDA UNITED METHODIST CHURCH

Hilda United Methodist Church. "History." Accessed January 2015. http://www.hildaumc.org/history.htm.

"Hilda, Texas." *Texas Escapes Online Magazine*. Accessed January 2015. http://www.texasescapes.com/TexasHillCountryTowns/Hilda-Texas.htm.

GRACE EPISCOPAL CHURCH

Brown, Lawrence L. "Protestant Episcopal Church," *Handbook of Texas Online* http://www.tshaonline.org/handbook/online/articles/iep01, accessed September 10, 2015. Uploaded on June 15, 2010. Published by the Texas State Historical Association.

BETHLEHEM LUTHERAN

"Quihi, Texas." *Texas Escapes Online Magazine*, last modified May 6, 2011. http://www.texasescapes.com/TexasHillCountryTowns/Quihi-Texas.htm.

TxGenWeb, Medina County. "Bethlehem Lutheran Church." http://www.rootsweb.ancestry.com/~txmedina/historic_sites.htm.

FIRST UNITED METHODIST CHURCH

Ford, Nora Mae, and Melba Schwertner. "First United Methodist Church of Bartlett, Historical Narrative." Williamson County Historical Commission. Accessed February 2015. http://www.williamson-county-historical-commission.org/Bartlett_Texas/First_united_Methodist_Church_of_Bartlett_Historical_Marker_Barlett_Texas.html.

ART METHODIST CHURCH

Cox, Mike. "History of Art." *Texas Escapes Online Magazine*. Accessed March 2015. http://www.texasescapes.com/TexasHillCountryTowns/ArtTexas/ArtTexas.htm.

ST. JOHN'S LUTHERAN CHURCH

Nienke, William, and Sam Morrow. "St. John's Lutheran Church—Fredericksburg, Gillespie County, Texas." Accessed March, 2015. http://www.9key.com/markers/marker_detail.asp?atlas_number=5171010106.

Kohout, Martin Donell. "Crabapple, TX," *Handbook of Texas Online* http://www.tshaonline.org/handbook/online/articles/hvcae, accessed September 10, 2015. Uploaded on June 12, 2010. Published by the Texas State Historical Association.

The Friends of Gillespie County Country Schools. "St. John Lutheran Church at Crabapple." Accessed April 2015. http://www.historicschools.org/stjohn.php.

SAINT LOUIS CATHOLIC CHURCH

Saint Louis Catholic Church. "History of St. Louis Church." Accessed April 2015. http://stlouischurchcastroville.org/history.php.

"St. Louis Catholic Church and Cemetery." *Texas Escapes Online Magazine*. Accessed April 2015. http://www.texasescapes.com/TexasHillCountryTowns/CastrovilleTexas/St-Louis-Catholic-Church-Castroville-Texas.htm.

TRINITY UNITED METHODIST CHURCH

"Castell, Texas." *Texas Escapes Online Magazine*. Accessed March 2015. http://www.texasescapes.com/TexasHillCountryTowns/Castell-Texas.htm.

SAINTS PETER AND PAUL CATHOLIC CHURCH
NEW BRAUNFELS

Goff, Myra Lee Adams. "Sts. Peter and Paul church family relations go back generations." Around the Sophienburg, February 9, 2014. http://sophienburg.com/blog?p=2231.

Waymarking.com. "The Church of Saints Peter and Paul—Texas Historical Markers." Accessed April 2015. http://www.waymarking.com/waymarks/WMFEKC_The_Church_of_Saints_Peter_and_Paul.

Saints Peter and Paul Catholic Church—New Braunfels, TX. "Parish History." Accessed April 2015. http://www.sppnb.org/parish-history.

SAINT MARY'S CATHOLIC CHURCH

Knopp, Kenn. "A Short History of New St. Mary's Church." KLRU: The Painted Churches of Texas: Echoes of the Homeland. Accessed March 2015. http://www.klru.org/paintedchurches/fredericksburg.html

Kohout, Martin Donell. "Vereins-Kirche," *Handbook of Texas Online* http://www.tshaonline.org/handbook/online/articles/ccv01, accessed September 10, 2015. Uploaded on June 15, 2010. Published by the Texas State Historical Association.

Brister, Louis E. "Adelsverein," *Handbook of Texas Online* http://www.tshaonline.org/handbook/online/articles/ufa01, accessed September 10, 2015. Uploaded on June 9, 2010. Published by the Texas State Historical Association.

Zion Lutheran Church

Wikipedia. "Zion Lutheran Church—Fredericksburg, Texas." Last modified September 5, 2015. https://en.wikipedia.org/wiki/Zion_Lutheran_Church_(Fredericksburg,_Texas).

Zion Lutheran Church. "The History of Zion Lutheran Church." Accessed March 2015. http://www.zion-lutheran.com/faqs/the-history-of-zion-luthera.html.

Kohout, Martin Donell. "Fredericksburg, TX," *Handbook of Texas Online* http://www.tshaonline.org/handbook/online/articles/hff03, accessed September 11, 2015. Uploaded on June 12, 2010. Published by the Texas State Historical Association.

EAST TEXAS

Zion Hill First Baptist

Stephen F. Austin State University, Center for Regional Heritage Research. "Diedrich Rulfs." Accessed April 2015. http://www.sfasu.edu/heritagecenter/7039.asp.

City of Nacogdoches. "Zion Hill Baptist Church." Accessed March 2015. http://www.ci.nacogdoches.tx.us/index.aspx?NID=882.

Old North Baptist Church

Pritchett, Bonnie. "Oldest Baptist church in Texas: small in number, big in faith, *Southern Baptist Texan*, October 10, 2006. http://www.bpnews.net/bpnews.asp?ID=24138.

Hesler, Samuel B. "Old North Baptist Church," *Handbook of Texas Online* http://www.tshaonline.org/handbook/online/articles/cc005, accessed September 11, 2015. Uploaded on June 15, 2010. Published by the Texas State Historical Association.

Jerusalem Memorial Christian Methodist Church

Visit San Augustine. "Historic Churches." Accesed November 2014. http://visit.sanaugustinetx.com/churches/jmcme.html.

Christ Episcopal Church

Wikipedia. "Frances Cox Henderson." Last modified February 12, 2015. http://en.wikipedia.org/wiki/Frances_Cox_Henderson.

Visit San Augustine. "Historic Churches." Accessed November 2014. http://visit.sanaugustinetx.com/churches/cce.html.

First Presbyterian Church

UNT Libraries. "About this Photograph." Portal to Texas History. Accessed September 5, 2015. http://texashistory.unt.edu/ark:/67531/metapth10431.

HistoricTexas.net "First Presbyterian Church, Palestine." Accessed September 2014. http://www3.historictexas.net/anderson-county/first-presbyterian-church-palestine.

Sacred Heart Catholic Church

Sacred Heart Catholic Church. "History." Accessed September 2014. http://www.shpalestine.org/history.

Shelby Chapel

The USGenWeb Project. "Shelby Chapel Cemetery, Henderson County, Texas." Accessed October, 2014. http://rootsweb.ancestry.com/~txhender/Cemeteries/ShelbyChapel/ShelbyChapelCem.htm.

Cumberland Presbyterian

Nienke, William, and Sam Morrow. "Presbyterian Church—Jefferson, Marion County, Texas." Accessed March 2015. http://www.9key.com/markers/marker_detail.asp?atlas_number=5315008080.

Wikipedia. "Jefferson, Texas." Last modified August 31, 2015. http://en.wikipedia.org/wiki/Jefferson,_Texas.

Saint Joseph Catholic

Malak, Clara. "The Beginnings." Saint Joseph Catholic Church History, December 19, 1999. http://stjosephnewwaverlytx.net/About%20Us/St.%20Joseph%20History2.html.

On the Way to Texas. "History of St. Joseph's Church, New Waverly." http://tex-family.com/showmedia.php?mediaID=276.

Reeves Chapel

Harper, Jr., Cecil. "Reeves Chapel, TX," *Handbook of Texas Online* http://www.tshaonline.org/handbook/online/articles/hvr96, accessed September 11, 2015. Uploaded on June 15, 2010. Published by the Texas State Historical Association.

Saint Beulah Christian Methodist Episcopal Church

Nienke, William, and Sam Morrow. "Saint Beulah Christian Methodist Episcopal Church—Pittsburgh, Camp County, Texas." Accessed April 2015. http://www.9key.com/markers/marker_detail.asp?atlas_number=5063009808.

First Methodist Church

First United Methodist Church, Pittsburgh, Texas. "Church History." Accessed April 6, 2015. http://www.fumcpittsburg.com/about/church-history.

Union Missionary Baptist Church

Preservation Texas. "Union Missionary Baptist Church." Accessed February 2015. http://www.preservationtexas.org/endangered/union-missionary-baptist-church.

Collins Academy, A Program of the Today Foundation. "Preservation Texas Names Union Missionary Baptist Church in Jefferson to Annual List of Texas' Most Endangered Historic Places." Last modified March 11, 2013. http://www.collinsacademy.com/preservation-texas-names-union-missionary-baptist-church-in-jefferson-to-its-ninth-annual-list-of-texas-most-endangered-historic-places.

Caddo Lake National Heritage Area. "Historic Church Named Most Endangered." Accessed February, 2015. http://www.caddolake-nha.com/RTHL%20Narrative.pdf.

MISCELLANEOUS SITES

Willis, Jim. "The Churches of Flanders." James Edward Flanders. Accessed March 11, 2013. http://jrgkwillis.homestead.com/8page1.html.

Willis, Jim. "The Churches of Flanders, Chapter 8." James Edward Flanders. Accessed March 2015. http://jameseflanders.homestead.com/JEFChapter8.html.